Fiscal Policy under Low Interest

Fiscal Policy under Low Interest Rates

Olivier Blanchard

PIIE PETERSON INSTITUTE FOR
INTERNATIONAL ECONOMICS

The MIT Press
Cambridge, Massachusetts
London, England

The MIT Press would like to thank the anonymous peer reviewers who provided comments on drafts of this book. The generous work of academic experts is essential for establishing the authority and quality of our publications. We acknowledge with gratitude the contributions of these otherwise uncredited readers.

This book was set in Stone Serif by Westchester Publishing Services. Printed and bound in the United States of America.

Library of Congress Cataloging-in-Publication Data

Names: Blanchard, Olivier (Olivier J.) author.
Title: Fiscal policy under low interest rates / Olivier Blanchard.
Description: Cambridge, Massachusetts : The MIT Press, [2022] | Includes
   bibliographical references and index. | Summary: "A guide for fiscal
   policymakers in advanced economies to understand the appropriate policy
   response to an environment of high national debt and
   low interest rates"—Provided by publisher.
Identifiers: LCCN 2022017741 (print) | LCCN 2022017742 (ebook) |
   ISBN 9780262544870 (paperback) | ISBN 9780262372756 (epub) |
   ISBN 9780262372961 (pdf)
Subjects: LCSH: Fiscal policy. | Social policy. | Interest rates. | Debts, Public.
Classification: LCC HJ192.5 .B53 2022 (print) | LCC HJ192.5 (ebook) | DDC
   332.4/15—dc23/eng/20220804
LC record available at https://lccn.loc.gov/2022017741
LC ebook record available at https://lccn.loc.gov/2022017742

10 9 8 7 6 5 4 3 2

To Bob Solow

Contents

List of Figures

Preface

"When the facts change, I change my mind. What do you do, sir?" (This statement is usually attributed to Keynes, but without hard proof that he actually said it.) This book was indeed triggered by facts changing–namely, by the steady decrease in real interest rates that started in the mid-1980s. Over time, I came to the conclusion that this was a fundamental change, one that was likely to last, although not without bumps along the way (and I shall come back to those in the book). And that this change forced us to rethink the role of fiscal and monetary policy.

The purpose of this book is to focus on the implications of low rates for fiscal policy, to review the theory and the evidence, and to draw practical implications for policy in advanced economies today.[1]

My target readers are primarily policy-makers and their staff who have to navigate complex waters over the coming years. They are the ones that I want and need to convince. The main challenge in discussing fiscal policy is the widely held and nearly religious belief that public debt is very bad. You can see this book as an attempt to take a richer and more balanced position. Not to love debt, but to understand when and how to use it.

The book is more of an essay than a treatise. There are still many questions to which I do not have a full answer, and some to which I am not even sure I have the right answer. The discussion covers a wide range of complex and often unsettled macroeconomic issues, from dynamic inefficiency to the source of the equity premium, the way quantitative easing

---

1. Translating these conclusions to emerging markets and developing economies is important but would have required an extensive treatment, which I decided not to explore in this book. For a first pass on commonalities and differences between advanced economies and emerging markets in this respect, see Blanchard, Felman, and Subramanian 2021.

works (or does not work), the nature of sudden stops, and the size of multipliers. I have tried to identify the zones of uncertainty or disagreement. I have tried to explain things simply in the text, being more precise in the boxes: some readers may find the treatment too difficult and others, too superficial. So be it.

One final remark added as I read the galleys in June 2022. I finished writing the book at the end of 2021. Since then, inflation has increased, and central banks are increasing nominal rates. Real rates are still extremely low, but they will increase further. As the readers will see, I had largely anticipated these evolutions, and explained why I thought they might lead to a temporary bump in rates but with a return to low real rates after that. I stand by these conclusions.

Thanks are due to an unusually large number of people.

First, I must mention my coauthors on fiscal policy issues throughout the years: Giovanni Dell'Ariccia, Rudi Dornbusch, Stanley Fischer, Jason Furman, Francesco Giavazzi, Alvaro Leandro, Daniel Leigh, Roberto Perotti, Jean Pisani-Ferry, Arvind Subramanian, Takeshi Tashiro, Angel Ubide, and Jeromin Zettelmeyer. Special thanks are due to Larry Summers; our discussions over nearly five decades have been always illuminating.

Second, I extend thanks to the many people who have offered suggestions and made comments on the first draft of the book: Silvia Ardagna, Agnès Bénassy-Quéré, Lorenzo Bini-Smaghi, John Cochrane, Peter Diamond, Carlo Favero, Joe Gagnon, Olivier Garnier, Vitor Gaspar, Jose de Gregorio, Martin Hellwig, Patrick Honohan, Gerhard Illing, Bas Jacobs, Larry Kotlikoff, Arvind Krishnamurthy, Paul Krugman, N. Greg Mankiw, Philippe Martin, Atif Mian, Emi Nakamura, Maury Obstfeld, Roberto Perotti, Jean Pisani-Ferry, Adam Posen, Jim Poterba, Xavier Ragot, Klaus Regling, Ricardo Reis, Chang Yong Rhee, Antonio Spilimbergo, Coen Teulings, Paul Tucker, Angel Ubide, Annette Vissing-Jorgensen, Etienne Wassmer, Christian von Weizsacker, Jakob von Weizsacker, Ivan Werning, and Charles Wyplosz. Special thanks to David Wilcox, who read the manuscript line by line and made it much better.

Third, I thank many of my colleagues from the Peterson Institute for International Economics who agreed to be part of a reading group. In addition to those already cited, the reading group included Jacob Kirkegaard and Madi Sarsenbayev, together with Michael Falkenheim, Kyoung Mook Lim, and John Seliski, from the Congressional Budget Office and Raphael

Espinosa and Daniel Leigh from the International Monetary Fund. I also thank the two anonymous referees who reviewed the book for MIT Press.

Fourth, I wish to acknowledge the many people who offered comments on the draft of the book available on the MIT Press open-source platform, among them Vivek Arora, Michael Ben-Gad, Johannes Brumm, Francesco Franco, Egor Gornostay, Yusuke Horiguchi, Richard Katz, Michael Kiley, Galo Nuno, Gabriel Patterson, Atanas Penakov, Jemima Peppel-Srebrny, John Quiggin, Lars Svensson, Gian Maria Tomat, Charles-Henri Weymuller, and Stavros Zenios. (I cannot thank MIT Press enough for providing such a free open site; not only has it increased the early visibility of the book and helped contribute to the current debate and policy decisions, but many of the comments pointed to mistakes or contributions that I was unaware of, and which I am able to correct in the final draft.)

Fifth, I want to thank an outstanding group of research assistants on this and earlier related projects: Gonzalo Huertas, Michael Kister, Julien Maire, and Thomas Pellet.

Sixth, my thanks to Adam Posen and the Peterson Institute for International Economics, which has provided me with a great working environment.

Finally, to Noelle, who has allowed me, once more, to obsess about the book and ignore all other tasks.

As usual, all mistakes are mine. And all the loose ends naturally determine my future research agenda.

Olivier Blanchard
Washington, DC
June 2022

1 Introduction

It is an understatement to say that policymakers in advanced economies face an unusual fiscal environment. The basic numbers are given in table 1.1 for seven major countries (as of the time of writing in January 2022). Net debt ratios are historically high, in most countries above 100%; except for Germany, they are substantially higher than they were in 2007, the year before the Global Financial Crisis. Deficit ratios are also extremely high; they largely reflect the lasting effects of the Covid crisis, but they were already fairly large in 2019, before Covid, in particular in the United States and in Japan. At the same time, nominal interest rates are extremely low; three-month rates on government bonds are often negative and 10-year rates are very low. In all cases, 10-year nominal rates are below expected inflation, implying negative real rates.

This has led policy-makers and academics to often reach drastically different conclusions about what fiscal policy should do at this juncture. Some, focused on the very high levels of debt, have argued for a need for urgent fiscal consolidation and a steady decrease in debt. Some have argued that it is enough to stabilize the debt and accept these higher levels. Some, focused on the very low rates, have argued that this is a great time for governments to borrow, especially if this is done to finance public investment. Yet others have argued for more radical solutions—for example, the cancellation of the debt held by central banks.[1]

---

1. Some notable comments come from Wolfgang Schäuble: "Borrowing in times of crisis to stabilise the economy makes sense, as long as the question of repayment is not forgotten. The need to pay back the debt later is often overlooked" (*Financial Times*, June 2, 2021); Paul Krugman: "The bottom line is that government debt just isn't a major problem these days" (*New York Times*, December 3, 2020); and a manifesto by 150 French economists: "Let's agree to a contract between European states

Table 1.1
Debt, deficits, and interest rates

Country	Net debt (% GDP)		Overall balance (% GDP)		Interest rate[a] (%)	
	2021[b]	2007[b]	2021[b]	2019[b]	10 yr.	3 mo.
US	101.9	45.5	−10.8	−5.7	1.7	0.2
Germany	54.4	53.4	−6.8	1.5	−0.0	−0.7
France	103.3	58.0	−8.9	−3.1	0.3	−0.7
Italy	142.2	95.7	−10.2	−1.6	1.3	−0.6
Spain	104.5	22.4	−8.6	−2.9	0.7	−0.6
UK	97.2	36.5	−11.9	−2.3	1.2	0.2
Japan	171.5	94.4	−9.0	−3.1	0.2	−0.1

[a] Interest rates are for January 28, 2022.
Source: Investing.com.
[b] The net debt numbers for 2021 are October forecasts for the end of the year.
Source: IMF Fiscal Monitor, October 2021.

What policymakers conclude and do will soon matter a lot. Many believe that in the wake of the Global Financial Crisis, the desire to decrease debt and the resulting fiscal consolidation were too strong, leading to a slower recovery. Policymakers in Europe now face a very concrete issue: Amid the Covid crisis, current EU fiscal rules have been suspended. The old rules are largely seen as in need of serious reforms. European Union policy makers have to redesign them in the right way.

The rest of this chapter offers a guided tour of the book and its major conclusions. It is simply a compendium of the introductions to each chapter.[2] Thus, think of it as Cliffs Notes for the hurried reader. If you are really in a hurry, the basic theme of the book is summarized in the very last chapter. If you actually intend to read the whole book, you may want to go directly to the chapters themselves.

Chapter 2 introduces five notions related to interest rates, which will be useful throughout the book.

---

and the ECB [European Central Bank]: The ECB commits to forgive the public debts that it holds, and the states agree to invest the same amounts in ecological and social reconstruction" (*Le Monde*, February 5, 2021).
2. I know this is rather unusual. But I have learned how we all have too much to read and how limited attention spans (at least my own) have become.

One is the neutral interest rate, r^*,[3] which can be defined in two equivalent ways. The first is that it is the safe real interest rate such that saving is equal to investment, assuming output is equal to potential output. The second is that it is the safe real interest rate such that aggregate demand is equal to potential output. The two definitions are indeed equivalent but suggest different ways of thinking about the factors that determine the neutral rate, and each will turn out to be useful later.

A second notion is the distinction between safe rates and risky rates such as the rate of return on stocks. It shows how an increase in perceived risk or in risk aversion leads to both a higher risky rate and a lower safe rate. When looking at data in chapter 2 and thinking about the factors behind low safe rates, the distinction will turn out to be empirically important. Are current low safe rates the result of shifts in saving or investment, or instead higher risk or risk aversion?

Third is the role of central banks. One can think of the effective mandate of central banks as setting the actual safe real interest rate, r, as close as they can to the neutral interest rate, r^*, and in so doing, keep output close to potential output. The important conclusion is that while central banks are sometimes blamed for the current low rates, the rates set by central banks reflect mostly low neutral rates, which themselves reflect the factors behind the movements in r^*, saving, investment, risk, and risk aversion. In other words, central banks are not to blame for low rates: these low rates just reflect underlying fundamental factors.

A fourth notion is the importance of the inequality $(r - g) < 0$, where r is the real safe interest rate and g is the real growth rate of the economy. When r is less than g, debt, if not repaid, accumulates at rate r while output grows at rate g. Thus, if no new debt is issued, the ratio of debt to output will decrease over time, making for more favorable debt dynamics. As r is forecast to be less than g with high probability for some (long) time to come, this will play a major role in our discussion of fiscal policy later.

A fifth discussion related to interest rates concerns the nature and implications of the effective lower bound (ELB). Because people can hold cash,

3. The neutral interest rate is also called the natural interest rate, following Wicksell 1936. But, like the natural rate of unemployment, it is in no way natural, depending on behavior and institutions. I shall therefore use the term neutral throughout.

which has a nominal interest rate of zero, central banks cannot decrease the nominal policy rate much below zero. This implies that they cannot achieve real policy rates much lower than the negative of inflation; call that rate the ELB rate and denote it by r_{min}. This potentially reduces their ability to decrease r in line with r^* when r^* is very low, leading to situations where $r > r^*$. In other words, it potentially reduces or even eliminates the room for monetary policy to maintain output equal to potential output. This is the situation in which many central banks have often found themselves in the recent past, and it again has major implications for our discussion of fiscal policy later.

The concluding section of chapter 2 notes that as the neutral rate r^* has declined over time, it has crossed two important thresholds. First, r^* and, by implication, r have become smaller than g, with important implications for debt dynamics and welfare effects of fiscal policy. Second, in some cases, r^* has become so low as to be lower than the ELB rate, r_{min}, limiting the room for monetary policy to maintain output at potential and, by implication, increasing the need to use fiscal policy.

Chapter 3 looks at the past evolution of interest rates. It is organized in four sections.

The first section looks at the evolution of safe real rates over time. It shows that, even ignoring the high real rates of the mid-1980s, which were largely the result of disinflationary policies followed by central banks, safe real rates have steadily declined across advanced economies, the United States, the euro zone, and Japan over the last 30 years. Their decline is due neither to the Global Financial Crisis of the late 2000s nor to the current Covid crisis, but to more persistent factors.

Second, the chapter shows that this decrease has led to an increasing gap between growth rates and safe rates, an increasingly negative value of $(r - g)$. While potential growth has slightly declined, the decrease in interest rates has been much sharper. While there have been periods of negative $(r - g)$ in the past, this one looks different, neither because of wars, nor bursts of inflation under low nominal rates, nor financial repression.

The chapter's third section looks at the potential factors behind the decline in safe rates. Different factors have different effects on saving/investment and on riskless/risky rates. Saving/investment factors affect all rates roughly in the same way. Risk/liquidity factors lead to lower safe rates and higher risky rates. The evidence is that both sets of factors have been at play. Within each set, the list of suspects is long, but their specific role is hard to pin down. I look more closely at two of the potential factors, where I have found the discussion to be misleading in the first case and confused in the second case.

When examining the relation between growth rates and interest rates, there is a wide belief that the two are tightly linked. Indeed, some of the research has been based on a relation known as the "Euler equation," a relation between *individual* consumption growth and the interest rate derived from utility maximization, which implies a close link between the two. I argue that this relation, however, has no implication for the relation between *aggregate* consumption growth (or output growth) and the interest rate. Indeed, and perhaps surprisingly, the empirical relation between the two is typically weak and often nonexistent. Lower potential growth is not the main cause of lower rates.

Turning to demographics, three major evolutions have been at work in advanced economies—namely, a decrease in fertility, an increase in life expectancy, and the passing effect of the baby boom. Some researchers have made the argument that these evolutions are partly behind low rates but will reverse as we look forward, leading to higher rates in the future. I argue that the future is likely to be dominated by the increase in life expectancy, and this is likely to further decrease interest rates rather than increase them.

The overall evidence suggests that the long decline in safe interest rates stems from deep underlying factors that do not appear likely to durably reverse in the future. The conclusion must, however, be qualified in two ways. The first is that we do not have a precise-enough sense of the factors behind the decline to be sure, and that fiscal policy must therefore be designed under the assumption of a small but positive probability of a sustained reversal. The second is that the future path of interest rates is not exogenous and depends very much on fiscal policy itself. Indeed, we are in the middle of an episode where a strong US fiscal expansion in 2021 is forcing the Fed to increase interest rates for some time so as to reduce aggregate demand and decrease inflation. This increase should, however, eventually fade away as inflation returns to its target level. I discuss this episode and its implications at more length in chapter 6. Looking beyond this episode, an increase in public investment, or continuing large deficits, may increase the neutral rate even in the long run. As I shall discuss in later chapters, fiscal policy should indeed be designed so as to achieve a value of r^* that allows central banks no longer to be tightly constrained by the ELB. If such a fiscal policy were to be implemented, it would imply a floor on future values of r^* and, by implication, on future values of r itself.

With the ground having been prepared, the next three chapters turn to the implications of low interest rates for fiscal policy. There are two separate questions to be answered, which are sometimes mixed up:

• How much "fiscal space" does a country have? Or more precisely, how much room does the country have to increase its debt until this raises issues of debt sustainability?

• How should this fiscal space be used? The fact that there is space does not mean that it should be used. Fiscal policy is about whether, when, and how to use that space.

Chapter 4 is about the first question. It starts with the arithmetic of debt dynamics *under certainty*, focusing on the role of $(r - g)$. The respective roles of $(r - g)$, debt, and primary balances are addressed, along with some of the dramatic implications of $(r - g < 0)$: Governments can run primary deficits and keep their debt ratios stable. Formally, there is no issue of debt sustainability. Whatever primary deficits governments run, debt may increase but it will not explode. Put another way, governments appear to have infinite fiscal space.

However, this conclusion is too strong, for two reasons. First, fiscal policy, in the form of higher debt or deficits, increases aggregate demand and thus increases the neutral rate r^*. To the extent that the monetary authority adjusts the actual rate r in response to r^*, this increases $(r - g)$ and thus reduces fiscal space. Second, uncertainty is of the essence. Debt sustainability is fundamentally a probabilistic concept. A tentative operational definition might go as follows: Debt is sustainable if the probability of a debt explosion is small (one still must define "explosion" and "small," but this can be done). With this in mind, the chapter discusses the various sources of uncertainty and their potential effects on debt sustainability. It shows the respective roles of the debt ratio, the maturity of the debt, the distribution of current and future primary balances, and the distribution of current and future $(r - g)$. It shows how "stochastic debt sustainability analysis" (SDSA) can be used by governments, investors, and rating agencies. It shows how realistic reductions in debt from current levels have little effect on the probability that debt is sustainable; in contrast, it shows the importance of contingent plans in case $(r - g)$ increases and durably reverses sign.

The chapter then looks at the case for fiscal rules to ensure debt sustainability. SDSAs can only be done in situ, for each year, for each country. The assumptions they require—for example, about the future evolution of $(r - g)$—leave room for disagreement. Can one design second best and more mechanistic rules as guardrails and still leave enough room for fiscal policy to perform its macroeconomic role? This is the question currently under discussion in the European Union. I express skepticism that any mechanistic rule can work well, but, if a rule is nevertheless going to be adopted, I suggest the direction it should explore. I argue that my analysis suggests a rule that adjusts the primary balance in response to debt service—rather than debt—over time.

Another topic covered in chapter 4 is the relation between public investment—for example, green investment—and debt sustainability. For political reasons, fiscal austerity has often led to a decrease in public investment rather than in other forms of spending. The transparency case for separating the current account and the capital account (known as "capital budgeting") is a strong one. The case for full debt financing of public investment, which is sometimes made, is however weaker: To the extent that public investment generates direct financial returns to the government, it can indeed be at least partially financed by debt without affecting debt sustainability. One may also argue that, by increasing growth, it increases future fiscal revenues. But much of public investment, even if it increases social welfare, does not generate financial returns for the state and has uncertain effects on growth. Thus, it can affect debt sustainability, and this must be taken into account in the way it is financed. I show how this can be integrated in an analysis of debt sustainability.

It is also important to look at the risk of sudden stops and the potential role of central banks in that context. Sovereign debt markets (and many other markets as well) are subject to sudden stops in which investors either drop out or ask for large spreads even in the absence of correspondingly large changes in fundamentals. This has been more of an issue in emerging economies' markets, but, as the euro crisis has shown, it is also relevant for advanced economies. Even if fundamentals suggest little debt sustainability risk and justify low rates, another equilibrium may arise where investors worry and ask for a spread over safe rates, increasing debt service and increasing the probability that debt is unsustainable, which ends up justifying their worries in the first place. Given its nature, this equilibrium is often referred to as a "sunspot equilibrium." I argue that the issue is relevant but that it would take extremely low levels of debt to eliminate the scope for multiple equilibria, levels far below current debt levels. Realistic reductions of debt over the next decades will not eliminate this risk.

I then look at whether central banks can reduce or even eliminate this risk. I distinguish between two sources for the increase in spreads: sunspots or deteriorations in fundamentals. I argue that central banks, by being large stable investors, can prevent multiple equilibria and eliminate spreads that are due to sunspots, but that the conclusion is less obvious when spreads are due, at least in part, to deteriorated fundamentals. The reason, in short, is that central banks are parts of the consolidated government and their interventions change the composition but neither the size of the overall consolidated government liabilities nor the overall risk. I discuss why this may be different in the case of the European Central Bank (ECB)—for example, in its ability to decrease Italian spreads during the Covid crisis.

Bailouts and write-offs are two issues that have come up in the relation of central banks to debt sustainability. Some observers have argued that through quantitative easing (QE) and the large-scale purchases of government bonds, central banks are monetizing the deficits and bailing out governments. I argue that this is not the case. Others have argued that to alleviate the debt burden, central banks should simply write off the government bonds they hold on their balance sheet. I argue that it is not needed, and if it were to be done, it would do nothing to improve the budget constraint of the government.

To summarize: Negative $(r - g)$ makes the dynamics of debt much more benign. This does not make the issue of debt sustainability disappear, both because of endogeneity (i.e., the effect of fiscal policy back on the neutral interest rate) and because of uncertainty, in particular with respect to r.

The best way to assess debt sustainability is through the use of SDSA, an approach that takes into account the specificities of each country and each year. Given the complexity of the assessment, I am skeptical that one can rely on quantitative rules. If, however, such rules are used, they should be based on requiring the primary surplus to adjust to debt service, defined as $((r - g)/(1 + g))b(-1)$, rather to debt itself. One cannot avoid including exceptions, however, such as the need to allow for larger primary deficits when the central bank is constrained by the ELB.

Chapter 5 looks at the welfare costs and benefits of debt and deficits and draws implications for fiscal policy. It begins with what may feel like an abstract and slightly esoteric topic but is actually central to the discussion of fiscal policy—namely, the effects of debt on welfare under certainty and then under uncertainty.

Consider the welfare costs of debt under certainty. Public debt is widely thought of as bad, akin to "mortgaging the future." The notion that higher public debt might actually be good and increase welfare (on its own, by ignoring what it is used to finance) feels counterintuitive. So, I review what we know about the answer under the assumption of certainty. The answer is that debt might indeed be good and that the condition, under certainty, is precisely $(r-g) < 0$. The answer has two celebrated steps: the "golden rule" result, from Phelps 1961, which says that if $(r-g) < 0$, less capital accumulation increases welfare; and the demonstration by Diamond 1965 in an overlapping generation model, which says that if $(r-g) < 0$, issuing debt does, by decreasing capital accumulation, increase the welfare of both current and future generations. These are clearly important and intriguing results. They are, however, just a starting point.

A major issue is again uncertainty. Under the assumption of certainty, there is only one interest rate, so the comparison between r and g is straightforward. But, in reality, there are many rates, reflecting their different risk characteristics. The safe rate is indeed less than the growth rate today. But the average marginal product of capital, as best as we can measure it, is substantially higher than the growth rate. Which rate matters? This is very much research in progress, but thanks to a number of recent papers, we have a better understanding of the issue. In the Diamond model, for example, which focuses on finite lives as the potential source of high saving and excess capital accumulation, the relevant rate is typically a combination of the two, although with a major role for the safe rate. Going to the data suggests that the relevant rate and the growth rate are very close, making it difficult to decide empirically which side of the golden rule we actually are. In other models where, for example, the lack of insurance leads people to have high precautionary saving, potentially leading to excess capital accumulation, the answer is again that the safe rate plays a major role; in that case, however, while debt is likely to help, the provision of social insurance, by getting at the source of the low r, may dominate debt as a way of eliminating capital overaccumulation. Overall, a prudent conclusion, given what we know, is that in the current context, public debt may not be good, but it is unlikely to be very bad—that is, to have large welfare costs: the more negative $(r - g)$, the lower the welfare costs.

Turning from costs to benefits, the main potential benefits of deficits and debt come from the role of fiscal policy in macro-stabilization, a central issue if, for example, monetary policy is constrained by the effective lower bound. I review what we know about the role of debt, spending, and taxes (and, by implication, deficits) in affecting aggregate demand: Higher debt affects wealth and thus consumption demand. Higher government spending affects aggregate demand directly; lower taxes do so by affecting consumption and investment. Multipliers—the effect of spending and taxes on output—have been the subject of strong controversies and a lot of recent empirical research, so there is also a discussion of what we have learned. The basic conclusion is that multipliers have the expected sign, and fiscal policy can indeed be used to affect aggregate demand.

When the conclusions about welfare costs and benefits of debt and deficits are put together, it is possible to draw their implications for fiscal policy. One can think of two extreme approaches to fiscal policy. The first, call it *pure public finance*, focuses on the role of debt and deficits, ignoring the effects of fiscal policy on demand and output by, for example, implicitly assuming that monetary policy can maintain output at potential in response to a change in fiscal policy. If this approach leads to the conclusion that debt is too high, then fiscal policy should focus on debt reduction. The second approach, call it *pure functional finance* (in reference to the name first used in Lerner 1943), focuses instead on the potential role of fiscal policy in maintaining output at potential, as might be the case if monetary policy is constrained by the effective lower bound. I argue that the right fiscal policy is a mix of these two approaches, with the weight on each one depending on the level of the neutral rate. The lower the neutral rate, the lower the fiscal and welfare costs of debt, on the one hand; the smaller the room of maneuver of the central bank, on the other; and thus the more the focus should be on the pure functional finance approach and on the use of deficits to sustain demand, even if it leads to an increase in debt. The higher the neutral rate, the higher the fiscal and welfare costs of debt, on the one hand; the larger the room of maneuver of the central bank, on the other;

and thus the more the focus should be on the pure public finance approach and, if indeed debt is perceived as too high, on a decrease in debt. A number of related issues are also discussed to round out the chapter, such as the role of the inflation target and alternatives to deficits to increase demand if secular stagnation becomes worse.

Chapter 6 looks at three episodes of fiscal policy in action. The chapter looks at three recent episodes where, for better or for worse, fiscal policy played or is playing a major role. The purpose is not to review each episode in full, which would take another book, but to show and discuss fiscal policy choices in the light of the analysis so far.

To caricature just a bit, the three episodes can be thought of "too little," "just right," and "too much."

Too little? The first case looks at the period of "fiscal austerity" that took place in the wake of the Global Financial Crisis. After the large initial increase in debt resulting from the crisis, the focus quickly turned to debt reduction. This was particularly true in the European Union, which embarked on a strong fiscal consolidation. Today, there is fairly wide agreement that, at least in Europe, the fiscal consolidation was too strong and relied too much on the traditional view of debt, both by markets and by policymakers, and came at a substantial output cost.

Just right? The second case looks at the Japanese economy over the last three decades. Japan experienced the ELB constraint starting in the mid-1990s, earlier than either the United States or Europe, and has remained close to it ever since. Japanese macroeconomic policy is often characterized as a failure, with the central bank unable to achieve its inflation target, with a low growth rate, and debt ratios steadily rising to reach more than 170% for net debt and 250% for gross debt. I think it should be seen instead as a qualified success, with the use of aggressive fiscal and monetary policies to compensate for very weak private demand: Output has remained close to potential. Growth is low, but because of demographics, not because of low productivity growth or high debt. Inflation is low, lower than the target, but this is not a major failure. Looking forward, however, there are reasons to worry: The debt ratios are very high. So far, investors do not mind, and 10-year nominal rates are close to zero. But can the buildup of debt continue? What happens if interest rates increase? Are there alternatives?

Too much? The third case looks at the effects of the *American Rescue Plan*, the stimulus program put in place by the Biden administration in early

2021. In 2020, the focus of fiscal policy had been protection of both house-holds and firms. In early 2021, the goal partially shifted from protection to sustaining the recovery. The size of the program was extremely large relative to the apparent output gap. The strategy (intentional or not) was in effect twofold: for the Treasury, to strongly increase aggregate demand and thus increase the neutral rate so as to relax the ELB constraint; and for the Federal Reserve, to delay adjustment of the policy rate to the neutral rate, allow for some overheating, and generate slightly higher inflation in the process. To a number of observers, including me, the size of the program appeared too large, leading to worries about overheating and excessive inflation. Exces-sive inflation may, in turn, force the Federal Reserve to increase interest rates so as to reduce inflation, and thus lead to a period of high nominal and real rates. I take stock of where things are, at the time of writing.

Chapter 7 concludes by summarizing the basic argument of the book and discussing what I see as the many issues that remain to be explored.

2 Preliminaries

Low interest rates are central to the story. With this in mind, the chapter introduces five notions related to interest rates, which will be useful throughout the book.

First is the neutral interest rate, r^*. It can be defined in two equivalent ways. The first is that it is the safe real interest rate such that saving is equal to investment, assuming output is equal to potential output. The second is that it is the safe real interest rate such that aggregate demand is equal to potential output. The two definitions are indeed equivalent but suggest different ways of thinking about the factors that determine the neutral rate, ways that will turn out to be useful later.

Second is the distinction between safe rates and risky rates such as the rate of return on stocks. It shows how an increase in perceived risk or in risk aversion leads to both a higher risky rate and a lower safe rate. Later, when looking at data in chapter 3 and thinking about the factors behind low safe rates, the distinction will turn out to be empirically important. Are current low safe rates due to shifts in saving or investment or instead to higher risk or risk aversion?

Third is the role of central banks in the determination of interest rates. The effective mandate of central banks is to set the actual safe real interest rate, r, as close as they can to the neutral interest rate, r^*, and in so doing, keep output close to potential output. The important conclusion is that while central banks are sometimes blamed for the current low rates, the rates set by central banks reflect mostly low neutral rates, which themselves reflect the factors behind the movements in r^*, saving, investment, risk, and risk aversion. In other words, central banks are not to blame for low rates: these just reflect underlying fundamental factors.

Fourth the importance of the inequality $(r - g) < 0$, where r is the real safe interest rate and g is the real growth rate of the economy. When r is less than g, debt, if not repaid, accumulates at rate r while output grows at rate g. Thus, if no new debt is issued, the ratio of debt to output will decrease over time, making for more favorable debt dynamics. As r is forecast to be less than g with high probability for some time, this will play a major role in our discussion of fiscal policy later.

Section 5 discusses the nature and implications of the effective lower bound (ELB). Because people can hold cash, which has a nominal interest rate of zero, central banks cannot decrease the nominal policy rate much below zero. This implies that they cannot achieve real policy rates much lower than the negative of inflation—call that rate r_{min}. This potentially reduces their ability to decrease r in line with r^* when r^* is very low, leading to situations where $r > r^*$. In other words, it potentially reduces or even eliminates the room for monetary policy to maintain output equal to potential output. This is the situation in which many central banks find themselves today, and again it has major implications for our discussion of fiscal policy later.

To summarize: The neutral rate r^* has declined over time, it has crossed two important thresholds. First, r^*, and by implication, r has become smaller than g, with important implications for debt dynamics and fiscal policy in general. Second, in some cases, r^* has become lower than the ELB rate r_{min}, limiting the room for monetary policy to maintain output at potential, and by implication, increasing the need to use fiscal policy.

2.1   The Neutral Interest Rate, r^*

Start with a much simplified view of what determines interest rates. Assume that there is just one interest rate, a real interest rate (i.e., a nominal rate minus expected inflation) such that saving is equal to investment. Write the equilibrium condition that saving equals investment as

$$S(Y, r, .) = I(Y, r, .), \tag{2.1}$$

where S is saving (which is assumed to depend on income Y, on the real interest rate r, and on other factors captured by the dot, which shift saving around) and I is investment (which also depends on output Y, on the real interest rate, r, and other factors captured by the dot, which shift investment around).

Note that, for simplicity, there is no explicit treatment of the role of the government here: Think of saving as capturing both private and government saving and investment as capturing both private and government investment. How fiscal policy affects saving and investment will be central and discussed at length later, but it is not essential to the point I want to make here. Note also that I ignore the fact that the economy may be open, so saving may not be equal to investment—although this has to be true for the world as a whole. I shall also return to the issue later when I discuss whether we should think of r^* as being determined by country-specific factors or by global factors.

Assume that output is equal to potential output, denoted as Y^*. Then, the equilibrium condition determines the value of the real rate such that saving is equal to investment; call it the *neutral rate* and denote it by r^*. Thus, r^* satisfies

$$S(Y^*, r^*, .) = I(Y^*, r^*, .). \tag{2.2}$$

The equilibrium is represented in figure 2.1, with saving and investment on the horizontal axis and the interest rate on the vertical axis. Both saving and investment are plotted against the interest rate, assuming $Y = Y^*$. Saving is increasing in the interest rate; investment is decreasing in the interest rate. The equilibrium is given by point A, with associated neutral rate r^*.

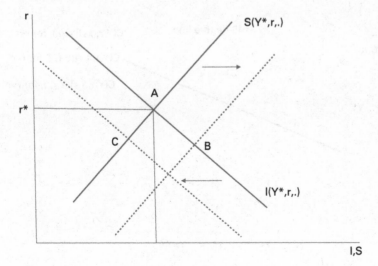

Figure 2.1
The determination of the neutral rate

This gives us a first definition of the neutral rate: *The neutral rate, r*, is the real interest rate at which, assuming output is equal to potential output, saving is equal to investment.*

A positive shift in saving shifts the saving relation to the right, shifting the equilibrium to point B, with higher saving and investment, together with a lower neutral rate. A negative shift in investment shifts the investment relation to the left, shifting the equilibrium to point C, with lower saving and investment, together with a lower neutral rate.

There is another, equivalent, way of looking at r^*, which will turn out to be useful as well. Define consumption $C = Y - S$, and rewrite the equation (2.1) as

$$Y = C(Y, r, .) + I(Y, r, .). \tag{2.3}$$

Output is equal to aggregate demand, the sum of consumption and investment (recall that consumption and investment include government consumption and government investment). Then, we can define r^* as the interest rate such that aggregate demand is equal to potential output, as follows:

$$Y^* = C(Y^*, r^*, .) + I(Y^*, r^*, .). \tag{2.4}$$

The equilibrium is represented in figure 2.2, with output on the horizontal axis and aggregate demand on the vertical axis, and it will be familiar

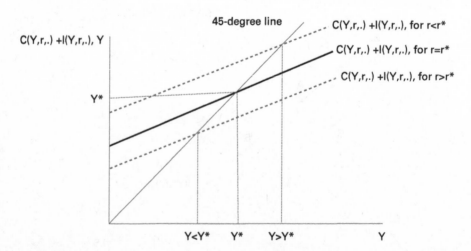

Figure 2.2
The determination of the neutral rate; an alternative representation

as a Keynesian cross diagram. Aggregate demand, $C+I$, is drawn as a function of Y for a given value of the interest rate r. $C+I$ is increasing in Y (and less than the 45-degree line, under the standard assumption that the sum of the marginal propensity to consume and the marginal propensity to invest is less than one); a higher interest rate decreases consumption and investment and shifts aggregate demand down; and a lower interest rate shifts aggregate demand up. For a given value of r, the equilibrium value of output is given by the intersection of $C+I$ and the 45-degree line ($Y = Y$). The neutral rate, r^* is such that the equilibrium level of output is equal to potential output Y^*. If r is greater than r^*, then aggregate demand is lower, and equilibrium output is lower than potential output, $Y < Y^*$; if r is lower than r^*, then aggregate demand is higher, and equilibrium output is higher than potential, $Y > Y^*$.

This gives us a second definition of the neutral rate: *The neutral rate, r^*, is the real interest rate such that aggregate demand generates output equal to potential output.*

Why two definitions, given that they deliver the same value of r^*? Because they naturally lead to a focus on different determinants of r^*:

• The first one leads to a focus on low-frequency determinants of saving and investment, such as demographics.

• The second leads to a focus on short-term determinants, such as the decrease in aggregate demand at the onset of the Global Financial Crisis or, thinking about fiscal policy, the increase in demand triggered by the stimulus package of early 2021 signed by President Joe Biden.

Both sets of factors are obviously important, and we shall explore them, and in particular the role of fiscal policy, later.[1]

---

1. The extensive literature on monetary policy typically defines r^* slightly differently than I do—for example, as a smooth version of my r^* or as the rate that keeps output at potential once the effects of shocks have worked themselves out (see Bomfim 1997 or Laubach and Williams 2003). The various econometric methods that these researchers then use to estimate r^*, the best known being that of Laubach and Williams, have the implication that the constructed series is smoother than my definition of r^*. Given this slow-moving r^*, researchers then explore alternative monetary policy rules such as the Taylor rule, which, in effect, react to deviations of short-run r^* from the smooth version of r^* or, equivalently, react to deviations of output from potential or/and to deviations of inflation from target inflation. For my purposes in this book, with its focus on fiscal rather than monetary policy, my

2.2   Safe Rates and Risky Rates, r and $r+x$

There are a lot of different interest rates and rates of return out there: safe/risky, short/long, rates on corporate/government bonds, rates of return on equities, housing, commodities, even bitcoin. It will be important later to introduce a distinction at least between safe and risky rates. So assume there are two rates, safe and risky. Assume saving depends on the safe rate (think of it as the interest rate on government bonds) and investment depends on the risky rate (think of it as the expected rate of return on equity). Denote the risky rate by $r+x$, where x represents the risk premium over the safe rate.[2]

In this case, the equilibrium condition takes the form

$$S(Y, r, .) = I(Y, r+x, .), \tag{2.5}$$

and the neutral safe rate is given by

$$S(Y^*, r^*, .) = I(Y^*, r^*+x, .). \tag{2.6}$$

The equilibrium is represented in figure 2.3, with the safe rate on the vertical axis and saving and investment on the horizontal axis. Given potential output, saving is an increasing function of the safe rate. Given potential output, investment is a decreasing function of the risky rate and thus, for a given risk premium, a decreasing function of the safe rate. The equilibrium is at point A, the safe rate is given by r^*, and by implication the risky rate is given by r^*+x.

An increase in the risk premium, call it $\Delta x > 0$, because of either higher risk or higher risk aversion, shifts the investment relation down by Δx and leads to a decrease in the safe rate of Δr^*; because the decrease in r^* is smaller than Δx, it leads to an increase in the risky rate.

So, this gives us another potential reason why the safe interest rate may be low (in addition to shifts in saving and investment that we saw

---

definition of r^*, together with the assumption that monetary policy aims at setting $r = r^*$, is a useful simplification.

2. If you want, you can think of financial intermediaries borrowing from individuals and offering them the safe rate and lending to firms at the risky rate. A more realistic but more complex formalization would assume that savers have the choice between safe and risky assets and that firms have access to risky investment and have to decide whether to finance it through a combination of safe and risky assets. The conclusions would be the same—namely, that an increase in risk or risk aversion leads to an increase in the risk premium and a decrease in the safe interest rate.

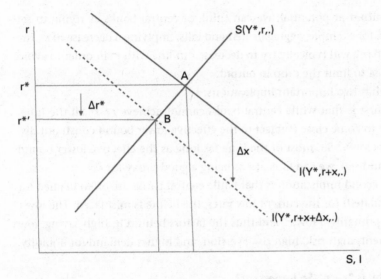

Figure 2.3
Safe rates, risky rates, and the risk premium

earlier)—namely, an increase in the risk premium due either to an increase in risk aversion or an increase in risk itself. A very similar argument holds if we think not of risk but of liquidity—and not of a risk premium on risky assets but a liquidity discount on safe assets. If we think of the asset paying the safe rate—for example, a Treasury bill—as more liquid and the other asset as being less so, an increased demand for liquidity will lead to a lower safe (liquid) rate and a higher rate on the less liquid one.

This gives us potentially four sets of factors to explain movements in the neutral rate: shifts in saving, shifts in investment, shifts in the risk premium, and shifts in the liquidity discount. I shall discuss what we know about their relative contributions in chapter 3.

2.3 The Role of Central Banks: Trying to Achieve $r = r^*$

The role of central banks is to avoid overheating, which might lead to increasing inflation, as well as underheating, which leads to excessive unemployment.[3] Given the definition of the neutral rate as the rate that

_____

3. This is not how their formal mandate is stated. For all central banks, their first formal mandate is to keep inflation low and stable. Many, but not all, also have a second mandate, which is in effect to keep output close to potential. Under plausible

keeps output at potential, we can think of central banks as trying to set $r = r^*$. If, for example, aggregate demand falls, implying a decrease in r^*, the central bank will typically try to decrease r in line with r^* in order to avoid or at least to limit the drop in output.

This has two important implications:

The first is that while central banks cannot achieve $r = r^*$ all the time, they try to come close (subject to the effective lower bound constraint discussed below).[4] So, most of the time (as long as the effective lower bound is not binding), we can look at r as being a good proxy for r^*.

The second implication is that while central banks are often blamed (or congratulated) for the current low rates, the blame is misplaced. The low r reflects primarily a low r^* and thus the factors behind it: high saving, low investment, high risk, high risk aversion, and higher demand for liquidity.

2.4   Why Is "$r < g$" So Important?

That the neutral rate r^*, and by the implication the actual rate r, could be very low was first discussed by Alvin Hansen (1939), who worried at the time that fewer and fewer investment opportunities would lead to low investment and weak private demand. He also believed that the interest elasticity of private demand was low (in terms of the IS-LM model, that the IS curve was very steep), implying that a low or even negative neutral rate might be needed to generate enough demand to maintain output at potential. He called such an outcome "secular stagnation."[5] In any event, his worries were not confirmed at the time, and private demand remained strong. Given recent evolutions, however, the same worries have reappeared, and in 2013, Lawrence Summers (2014) argued that we might indeed have entered

---

conditions, the two objectives are roughly consistent, as maintaining stable output at potential also yields stable inflation, an outcome known as the "divine coincidence" (Blanchard and Gali 2007).

4. There are likely to be large high-frequency swings in r^*, say, from month to month. It is clear that monetary policy cannot match all these swings, and it is not even clear that it should. But when we look at, say, movements in r over a year or longer, it is reasonable to assume that they approximate the underlying movements in r^*. I shall ignore these complications here. They are extremely important for the design of monetary policy, not so much for fiscal policy.

5. A nice history of the concept, from Hansen to Summers, is given by Backhouse and Boianovsky 2016.

a period of "secular stagnation" and that r was going to remain low for a long time. I am not sure that the Hansen-Summers terminology is best, but it has become standard (I would prefer the term "structurally weak private demand," but it probably sounds too technical).

As r^* has decreased over the last 30 years (much more on this in chapter 3), it has crossed two important thresholds. First, it became less than the growth rate: r^* and by implication r became lower than g. The second is that it became so low that, at times, monetary policy could not decrease r to match the decrease in r^*, a constraint known as the effective lower bound.

This section focuses on the implications of what happens when the safe real interest rate becomes less than the growth rate. For lack of a better label, I shall call it the $(r - g) < 0$ condition.[6] The inequality clearly holds today and, as I shall argue in chapter 3, is likely to hold for some time to come. (Here is a good place to clarify the relation between the statement that $r < g$, and the main point from Piketty 2014 that $r > g$. There is no contradiction as we are referring to different rates. Mine is the safe interest rate, which is indeed less than the growth rate; Piketty's is the risky rate, the average rate of return on wealth, which is indeed greater than the growth rate.)

The sign of $(r - g)$ indeed has strong implications for debt dynamics as well as for the welfare implications of debt.

Take debt dynamics first. For any borrower, a low interest rate is good news. But, if you or I borrow, we still must pay back the loan before we die. Governments do not need to do that. In effect, because they live forever, when debt becomes due they can issue new debt (i.e., "rollover debt"). All governments do that.

To see what this implies, start from a situation where the government has no initial debt and taxes are equal to spending, so the budget is balanced. Now suppose that the government increases spending for just one year, but it does not raise taxes and thus issues debt to finance the deficit. From the second year on, with spending back to normal, taxes again cover noninterest spending but not interest payments. Debt thus increases at rate r. Output, on the other hand, grows at rate g.[7]

If $r > g$, which has long been taken as the standard case, the ratio of debt to output, often called the "debt ratio" for short, will increase exponentially

---

6. In fact, "$(r - g) < 0$" has become sort of a household word among economists.
7. A detailed discussion of debt dynamics will be given in chapter 4.

at rate $(r-g)$, and sooner or later, if the government does not want the debt ratio to explode, it will have to increase taxes (or decrease spending, or both). But if $r < g$, the situation we are in today and expect to be in for some time to come, then the debt ratio will decrease over time. Indeed, if $r < g$ forever, then the government can spend more for a while, issue debt, and never raise taxes. Thus, the standard notion that higher debt implies the need for higher taxes in the future seems no longer to hold.

Turn to welfare implications. A low r is actually a signal that something is wrong with the economy: In effect, if we think of the safe rate as the risk-adjusted rate of return on capital, the low safe rate is sending the signal that, risk adjusted, the return on capital is low. Put another way, it is sending the signal that capital is in fact not very productive at the margin. If so, to the extent that we think of debt as crowding capital and thus decreasing capital accumulation, debt may not be costly. It may even be beneficial if there truly was too much capital to start with.

These are fairly dramatic results. If $r < g$ were really to hold forever, it would suggest a very relaxed attitude toward debt. As we shall see, it comes however with two strong caveats. First, debt and deficits increase aggregate demand and thus increase r^*; if central banks set $r = r^*$, then r increases, possibly changing the sign of the inequality and returning debt dynamics to the standard case. Second, we cannot be sure that $r < g$ will last forever (or at least for a very long time). And, if it does not, we have to think about what adjustment might be needed. Thus, a central question will be: What do we expect r and g to do in the future? This requires looking at history and at likely underlying factors and their likely future evolutions. This will be the topic of chapter 3. The implications for debt dynamics, for welfare, and for fiscal policy in general, will be the subject of the subsequent chapters.

2.5 Nominal and Real Rates and the ELB

I have assumed so far that central banks were able to set r equal to, or at least close to, r^*. So, in response to a sharp decrease in demand, leading to a sharp decrease in r^*, I assumed that they were able to decrease r to match the decrease in r^*. When r^* is very low, however, this may not be the case.

Historically, over the nine US recessions since 1960, the decrease in the (nominal) policy rate during recessions ranged from 2% to 8.8%, with an average decrease of 5%.[8] This was possible because inflation was, on average, much higher than today, and so were average nominal interest rates.[9]

With low inflation and low neutral real rates today, central banks have lost much of the room they had to decrease r in response to r^*. Central banks control directly the nominal rate, not the real rate. To a first approximation, nominal interest rates cannot go negative, a constraint known as the *zero lower bound* (ZLB).[10] This is because if they did, holding cash—which yields a nominal rate of zero—would become a superior alternative to holding bonds, and people would want to shift to cash. This has a simple but important implication.

Write down the relation between the real rate r, the nominal rate i, and the expected rate of inflation π^e:

$$r = i - \pi^e. \tag{2.7}$$

If the nominal interest rate cannot be negative, then the lowest the real rate can be is the negative of expected inflation, $-\pi^e$.[11] Depending on the country, today's forecasts of inflation by firms and investors over,

---

8. See Summers 2016, fig. 17. And the Fed would have decreased the rate much more in response to the Great Financial Crisis if it indeed had not been constrained by the zero lower bound, as we discuss below.

9. The Fisher effect suggests that, in the long run, the nominal rate reflects the real neutral rate plus the average inflation rate.

10. This situation is also referred to the "liquidity trap." When the nominal rate is down to zero, further increases in money (liquidity) no longer have an effect on the nominal rate: As bonds and money pay the same rate—namely, zero—people are indifferent to holding money or bonds. They are thus willing to exchange bonds for money without a change in the rate. Paul Krugman (1998) was one of the first researchers to emphasize the policy implications of the liquidity trap. His paper focused on monetary policy rather than fiscal policy implications. My focus will be more on the fiscal policy implications.

11. Actually, the relation between the nominal rate, the real rate, and expected inflation in the text is only an approximation, but it is a good one if expected inflation is low: If you hold a one-period bond that promises you $1+i$ dollars next period, then your expected real return is given by $(1+i)P/P^e$, where P is the price level this period and $P^e(+1)$ is the price level expected next period. Noting that $P/P^e(+1) = 1/(1+\pi^e)$, where π^e is expected inflation, this implies the following relation: $(1+r) = (1+i)/(1+\pi^e)$, or equivalently $r = (i-\pi^e)/(1+\pi^e)$. The expression in the text ignores the term $(1+\pi^e)$, which, unless inflation is very high, is very close to 1.

say, the next five years are around 2–3%, thus implying, if the nominal rate cannot be negative, a lower limit for the five-year real rate of minus 2–3%.[12]

Central banks have learned, however, that they can actually set slightly negative nominal rates without triggering a major shift to cash. This is because holding very large quantities of cash is inconvenient, potentially dangerous, and in some cases simply infeasible—for example, if banks sold their bond holdings and replaced them with cash, they would have to hold gigantic amounts of cash, at some security risk.[13] Thus, as was shown in table 1.1 in the introduction, a number of central banks have been able to set *negative* nominal rates—for example, at the date of this writing, −0.75% for the Swiss policy rate. To reflect this, the constraint on monetary policy is no longer called the zero lower bound but, rather, the *effective lower bound*. The additional room from negative nominal rates is small, however, relative to the required size of decreases in r in the past.[14]

The ELB has two clear implications for fiscal policy:

• If, as is the case at the time of writing, the ELB constraint is strictly binding in many advanced economies, and the output gap is still negative, there is no room for monetary policy to increase demand and output. Put another way, if r^* is less than r_{min}, central banks cannot get r down to r^*, and the burden of increasing demand to return output to potential must fall fully on fiscal policy.

• If, as is likely to happen at some point and will probably have happened when this book comes out, aggregate demand strengthens, leading to an

---

12. At the time of writing, there is a worry that fiscal stimulus in the United States may lead to overheating and an increase in inflation for some time, leading in turn to higher expected inflation and thus a lower limit for the real rate. The implications of the current stimulus program are discussed in chapter 6.

13. A billion dollars held in one-dollar bills would require about 1,129 cubic meters of space—for example, a box with sides of 10.4 meters. I agree that banks would not have to hold it in one-dollar bills.

14. Another tool in the toolbox of central banks is quantitative easing (QE), the purchase of long maturity bonds in order to decrease their yield. I shall return to QE issues at various points in the book. Like negative rates, QE has helped a bit, but not enough to give central banks sufficient room in response to a substantial decrease in r^*.

increase in r^* above the effective lower bound, then the ELB may no longer strictly bind, and most nominal interest rates will become positive again. But they are still unlikely to be high enough to allow central banks to react to large adverse shocks to demand. In that case, fiscal policy will have to be the main policy instrument to respond to the decrease in demand.

Before moving on to conclusions, I want to note an important conceptual difference between secular stagnation and the ELB constraint. Secular stagnation—that is, a very low r^*, leading to $(r - g) < 0$—reflects fundamental forces in the economy, which may not be easy to undo. The ELB constraint is instead more of a self-inflicted wound, or to use a soccer expression, an own goal. The low inflation rate of the last three decades reflects largely the target inflation rate chosen by central banks, typically around 2%.[15] Had central banks chosen a higher target, inflation would likely have been higher and so would have expected inflation; nominal rates would have been higher, and there would have been more room to decrease them, were it to be needed. The discussion of the right inflation target is a long one, and it is far from settled; but it often ignores the fact that, if the target is chosen too low and the ELB is often strictly or potentially binding, more of the macro-stabilization must be achieved through fiscal policy, which may have its own costs.[16]

2.6 Conclusions

We now have the tools we need to think about fiscal policy. And you can already see the basic implications of both $(r - g) < 0$ and the ELB constraint:

• To the extent that $r - g$ remains negative for a long time in the future, debt may not be very costly, either in fiscal terms or in welfare terms.

---

15. The Fed adopted an explicit inflation target of 2% in 2012. The choice of the target was thought to balance the costs of inflation and the benefits of inflation, among them a lower probability of hitting the ZLB. It is fair to say that most of the models then used to assess the trade-off underestimated the probability of hitting the ZLB.

16. Another way to relax the ELB constraint, suggested in particular by Kenneth Rogoff (2017), would be to ban cash. If we only had bank deposits, the rate on deposits could be negative and there would be no asset that dominates it. This is not feasible at this stage but may become more so in the future

• To the extent that the ELB constraint continues to bind, either strictly or potentially, fiscal policy (i.e., higher deficits) may be needed to maintain output at potential.

• This suggests an economic environment with lower costs of debt and higher (output) benefits of deficits (debt).

But what will happen to the neutral rate in the future? This is the topic of chapter 3.

3 The Evolution of Interest Rates, Past and Future

The chapter, organized in four sections, begins with a look at the evolution of safe real rates over time. Section 3.1 shows that, even ignoring the high real rates of the mid-1980s that were largely due to the disinflationary policies followed by central banks, safe real rates have steadily declined across advanced economies—the United States, the euro zone, and Japan—over the last 30 years. The decline in interest rates is due neither to the Global Financial Crisis of the late 2000s nor to the more recent Covid crisis, but is the result of more persistent factors.

This decrease has led to an increasing gap between growth rates and safe rates and, as a result, to an increasingly negative value of $(r-g)$. While potential growth has slightly declined, the decrease in interest rates has been much sharper. While there have been periods of negative $(r-g)$ in the past, this one looks different because it is not caused by wars, bursts of inflation under low nominal rates, or financial repression.

There are different potential factors behind the decline in safe rates. Different factors have different effects on saving/investment and on riskless/risky rates: Saving/investment factors affect all rates roughly in the same way. Risk/liquidity factors lead to lower safe rates and higher risky rates. The evidence is that both sets of factors have been at play. Within each set, the list of suspects is long, but their specific role is hard to pin down.

The chapter looks more closely at two of the potential factors, where I have found the discussion to be misleading in the first case and confused in the second case.

Section 3.2 looks at the relation between growth rates and interest rates. There is a wide belief that the two are tightly linked. Indeed, some of the research has been based on a relation known as the "Euler equation," a relation between *individual* consumption growth and the interest rate derived from utility maximization, which implies a close link between the two. I argue that this relation, however, has no implication for the relation between *aggregate* consumption growth (or output growth) and the interest rate. Indeed, perhaps surprisingly, the empirical relation between the two is typically weak and often nonexistent. Lower potential growth is not the main cause of lower rates.

Section 3.3 looks at the role of changing demographics. Three major demographic evolutions have been at work in advanced economies—namely, a decrease in fertility, an increase in life expectancy, and the passing effect of the baby boom. Some researchers have made the argument that these evolutions are partly behind low rates but will reverse as we look forward, leading to higher rates in the future. I argue that the future is likely to be dominated by the increase in life expectancy, and this is likely to further decrease rather than increase interest rates.

The overall evidence suggests that the long decline in safe interest rates stems from deep underlying factors that do not appear likely to reverse anytime soon. The conclusion must, however, be qualified in two ways. The first is that we do not have a precise enough sense of the factors behind the decline to be sure, and that fiscal policy must therefore be designed under the assumption of a small but positive probability of a sustained reversal. The second is that the future path of interest rates is not exogenous and depends very much on fiscal policy itself. For example, the 2021 stimulus package signed by President Joe Biden may well increase aggregate demand and, by implication, lead to higher r^* and r for a few years. As I shall discuss in later chapters, fiscal policy should indeed be designed so as to achieve a value of r^* that allows central banks to no longer be tightly constrained by the effective lower bound (ELB). If such a fiscal policy were to be implemented, it would imply a floor on future values of r^* and, by implication, on future values of r itself.

3.1   The Evolution of the Safe Rate

Figure 3.1 shows the evolution of 10-year real interest rates on sovereign bonds, constructed as the difference between 10-year nominal rates and 10-year forecasts of inflation, since 1992, in the United States, the euro zone, and Japan.

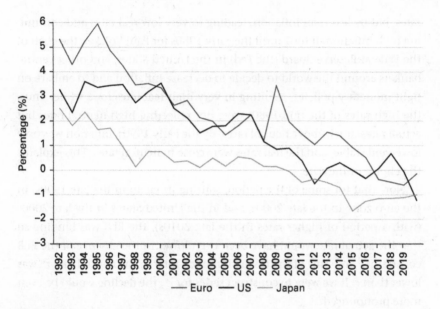

Figure 3.1

US, Euro, Japan 10-year real rates, 1992–2020.

Sources: US 10-year nominal rate on government bonds minus 10-year inflation forecasts are from the Survey of Professional Forecasters; Euro rates are from Schnabel 2021; Japan nominal 10-year rate minus 10-year inflation forecast is constructed from Adachi and Hiraki 2021, fig. 8.

Why look at these bonds? Because they are largely considered safe from default, so they are a good measure of the safe rate. Why 10-year rates? Because they are close to the average maturity of public debt and thus a good indicator of the average interest rate on public debt; the average maturity of debt is 7 years for the advanced country members of the Group of Twenty (G20), 7.8 years for France, 14.8 years for the United Kingdom, 5.8 years for the United States.[1]

Why start in 1992 and not earlier? Real rates were even higher in the early 1980s and peaked around 1985 in most advanced economies. Thus, the figure would be more even more striking if it started in 1985. It would, however, be misleading. To see why, one must go back to what happened in the 1970s. During that decade, increases in the price of oil and other commodities led to increasing inflation. Central banks increased nominal

---

1. IMF Fiscal Monitor, April 2021, table A23.

rates, but by less than inflation, leading to very low real rates and continuing high inflation. It took until the early 1980s for Paul Volcker, the chair of the Federal Reserve Board (the Fed) in the United States, and other central bankers around the world to decide to decrease inflation and to embark on tight monetary policies, resulting in very high real rates for a while. Thus, the high rates of the mid-1980s were not reflecting high neutral rates but actual rates much above neutral rates. By the early 1990s, inflation was now lower and stable, and the real rates were close to neutral rates. This explains the choice of the date.

Note that for some of the period, starting in Japan in the late 1990s, in the euro zone in the late 2000s, and in the United States in the late 2000s (with a period of higher rates in the late 2010s), the ELB was binding so that the actual rate would have been even lower in the absence of the ELB constraint.[2] In terms of the discussion in chapter 2, the neutral rate r^* was lower than r. If we were to construct series for r^*, the decline would be even more pronounced.

Figure 3.1 yields two major conclusions:

• While the decline started earlier in Japan (and for some time, it was seen as a Japan idiosyncratic evolution, until it caught up with the United States and the euro zone), it has been largely common to all three economies. This suggests either that the same forces were operating in all countries, or that financial markets are largely integrated, or more likely, a combination of the two.

• The decline has been steady and is not caused by either the Great Financial Crisis or the Covid-19 crisis. It started long before, and while the two crises led to lower neutral rates, only partly reflected in actual rates because of the ELB, they are hardly visible in the figure.

How historically unusual are such a steady decline and sustained low levels of real rates? Going back further in time, the lack of measures of inflation expectations makes it harder or impossible to construct ex ante real rates (i.e., nominal rates minus expected inflation); real-time forecasts do not exist, and econometric constructs are not as reliable. One can, however, easily compute ex post real rates (i.e., nominal rates minus realized inflation). Looking at the United States over the twentieth century, doing

---

2. The ELB constraint applies to the policy rate, which is a short rate. But, by implication, it also puts a lower limit on longer rates, such as the 10-year rate.

so shows that there indeed have been periods of low or negative ex post real rates. This was, for example, the case during World War II and its aftermath. In 1942, the Fed agreed to peg the Treasury bill rate at a very low level (0.375%) to allow the Treasury to finance war spending at low cost, a case of "fiscal dominance" of monetary policy. After the war, the economy boomed and inflation steadily increased, reaching 20% in February 1951, leading to extremely low real rates; at that point, the Fed and the Treasury agreed to stop the peg, and real rates recovered from 1952 on. As I mentioned earlier, this was also the case in the 1970s, when central banks kept rates too low in the face of higher inflation; this is now generally seen as a policy mistake that had to be undone through disinflation policies in the early 1980s. The current situation is very different from these episodes. In both earlier cases, the evidence suggests that, for different reasons in the two cases, the actual rate r was substantially lower than the neutral rate r^*. This is not the case today: If anything, the fact that the ELB is still binding in many countries implies that r is higher than r^*. Low rates are not the result of fiscal dominance or policy mistakes but very low neutral rates.

It is useful to take an even longer view, and for this, I shall rely on the work of Schmelzing (2020), who has constructed series for the safe real rate over seven centuries, starting with borrowing by Venice in the 1300s to borrowing by the US Treasury today.[3]

Figure 3.2 again shows a striking picture, with the safe rate decreasing from 10–15% in the 1300s to close to 0% today.[4] It suggests a strong underlying negative trend of about 1.2 basis points (bp) per year,[5] and thus deep, low-frequency forces at work (the estimated negative trend since 1992 is much stronger, about 15 bp per year in the United States, 20 in Japan, and 18 bp in the euro zone).

My conclusions from the evidence in this first section are twofold:

• The longer historical evidence suggests deep, low-frequency underlying forces at work.

---

3. Another long view is provided by Mauro and Zhou (2021), who put data together for 55 countries over 200 years. They find that ex post real rates have indeed often been less than growth rates, but as in the two US examples given in the text, most of the episodes suggest the role of fiscal dominance or monetary policy mistakes as the main culprits.

4. Because it is a centered moving average and the underlying series stops in 2018, the series stops in 2008.

5. A basis point (bp) is one-hundredth of a percent per year

Figure 3.2
Safe real rate since 1325.
Source: Schmelzing 2020.

- Something has happened in the last 30 years that is different from the past—even if one ignores the abnormally high rates of the mid-1980s.

The Dramatic Decline in $(r - g)$

As we saw in chapter 2, what is important for fiscal policy and debt dynamics is not so much r but $(r - g)$. Figure 3.3 shows the evolution of the US 10-year real rate (the same series as in figure 3.1) and the forecast 10-year real output growth rate, from the Survey of Professional Forecasters (SPF).[6,7]

The figure is again quite striking. Forecast US real growth went up in the 1990s, from 2.6% in 1992 to 3.3% in 2001, but has come down since

---

6. The series for 10-year forecasts of growth starts in 1992.
7. I could not find corresponding 10-year growth forecasts for other countries, but a rough pass at the data suggests that the conclusions would be similar to those for the United States.

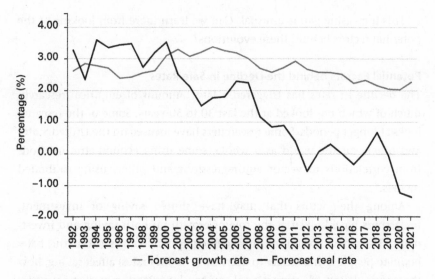

Figure 3.3

US 10-year real rate and forecast 10-year real output growth rate since 1992.
Source: Survey of Professional Forecasters (SPF) 10-year nominal yields minus SPF forecasts of 10-year inflation and SPF forecasts of 10-year real growth rates.

then and stood at 2.3% in 2021, thus just a bit lower than in 1992. The safe real rate, as we have seen earlier, has decreased substantially, and since 2000, $(r-g)$ has turned negative—and increasingly so. At the start of 2021 (the latest date for which there are forecasts), 10-year $(r-g)$ was equal to −3.2%.[8] Markets thus expected r to be substantially lower than g for the next 10 years; in fact, they expected it to hold for much longer. At the start of 2021, the rate on 30-year TIPS (that is, indexed bonds) was −0.4%. A reasonable forecast of real growth over the next 30 years might be 2%, implying a value of $(r-g)$ over the next 30 years of −2.4%.

---

8. One issue is that the two series do not use the same inflation measure. Real growth is equal to nominal growth domestic product (GDP) growth minus inflation using the GDP deflator. Real rates are constructed as nominal interest rates minus SPF forecasts of CPI (rather than GDP deflator) inflation. An alternative way of computing the difference between r and g, which does not suffer from this problem, is to compare nominal interest rates and forecasts of nominal GDP growth. At the start of 2021, 10-year nominal rates were equal to 1.3%, and 10-year nominal growth forecasts from Moody's Analytics (private communication) were equal to 4.5%, again implying a difference of 3.2%.

This increasing gap is unusual. Can we learn more from looking at the potential factors behind these evolutions?

Potential Factors behind the Decline in Safe Rates

The decline in rates has triggered a large amount of empirical research, much of which has looked at the last 30 to 50 years. Some of the research looks at longer periods. Some researchers have focused on the United States and others on the world as a whole, some using econometric methods from correlations to vector autoregressions and others using calibrated models.[9]

Among the factors that may have shifted saving or investment, researchers have looked at the role of growth on both saving and investment. They have examined how demographic changes (from the baby boom to people living longer to decreasing fertility rates) affect saving; how the accumulation of international reserves by emerging market countries affects saving; the role of increasing within-country inequality on saving; the effect that decreases in the price of capital goods and decreases in technological progress (the initial Alvin Hansen worry) have on investment; and importantly, the role of fiscal policy. On this point, Rachel and Summers (2019), in particular, have emphasized that fiscal policy, especially the substantial increase in debt ratios over the period (that we saw in table 1.1 earlier), probably led, other things being equal, to an *increase* in r^* during that period. Put another way, absent fiscal policy, the decline in r^* would have been even larger than it has been. This is an important point, both historically and prospectively: Forecasts of r^* must depend on what fiscal policies will be in the future.

Among the factors that may have shifted risk premia or liquidity discounts, researchers have looked at the role of increases in investors' risk aversion (often called "market risk aversion" to reflect the fact that it may depend on more than individual risk preferences). They have also examined the role of increases in risk itself coming from more complex processes of production; the role of increases in risk coming from a higher proportion

---

9. These models include Bernanke 2005; Rachel and Summers 2019; Summers 2016; Von Weizsacker and Kramer 2021; Haskel 2020; Platzer and Peruffo 2021; Eggertson, Mehrotra, and Robbins 2019; Mian, Straub, and Sufi 2021b; Caballero, Farhi, and Gourinchas 2017; Del Negro et al. 2019; Lunsford and West 2019; Kiley 2020; and Pethe 2021, among others.

of intrinsically more risky intangibles in investment; the role of increases in the demand for safe assets by emerging markets; the role of increases in the demand for safe and liquid assets coming from liquidity regulations in the wake of the Great Financial Crisis; the reassessment of what assets are truly safe, in light of the Global Financial Crisis; and the role of aging as older individuals, in particular retirees, tend to want safer portfolios.

The specific role of each of these factors, and whether their evolution might be different in the future compared with the past, deserves a full discussion but would go beyond what I can do here. My reading of this line of research is that, while these factors are indeed plausible suspects, their quantitative role is hard to pin down. Empirical work faces many challenges.

To state the first obvious difficulty, the variable we are trying to explain, r^*, is not directly observable, and the ELB, which cuts the link between r and r^*, complicates matters.

Then, there is the issue of what period one should look at. Rachel and Summers, for example, look at the period from 1970 to 2017, but the decrease in safe rates really only happened from the mid-1980s on, and as argued earlier, movements in r in the 1970s and early 1980s largely reflected deviations of r from r^*, which were negative in the 1970s, positive in the 1980s.

Yet another issue is the role of national versus global factors. When looking, for example, at saving as a determinant of r^* in a particular country, should one look at shifts in country saving or in world saving? The answer is a mix of the two, depending on the size of the country, the degree of international financial integration, and the permanent or temporary nature of the shifts. It is likely, for example, that the high saving rates and the resulting sustained large current account surpluses that China ran over the period increased world saving and led, other things being equal, to a lower r^* for the rest of the world.[10] In contrast, a temporary expansion of demand, such as that triggered by the Biden stimulus, even if it leads to an increase in r^* in the United States (an issue to which I shall return in chapter 6), may not lead to a similar increase in r^* in other countries. They may decide to deviate from the US r^* and let their exchange rate move accordingly.[11]

---

10. See Bernanke 2005.
11. A nice discussion of the role of global factors, exchange rates, and current account balances in the determination of national r^* is given by Obstfeld 2020.

In short, identifying the role of both domestic and global factors on saving, investment, risk, and risk perceptions is not easy. Reading the papers that have had the courage to try, one has a feeling of an abundance of riches, with too many explanatory variables and too few observations. Indeed, when the sample is extended, as done, for example, by Schmelzing 2018, few of the correlations between rates and potential explanatory variables appear robust. Thus, while the research points to the right set of suspects, few of them can be indicted, and estimates of their specific quantitative contributions must be taken with a grain of salt.[12]

I think one can, however, reach a few conclusions, especially on the relative role of saving/investment shifts versus the role of safety/liquidity factors. The discussion and the figures in chapter 2 give a way of looking at the data. A positive shift in saving should lead to higher saving and investment and a decrease in all rates, safe and risky.[13] An adverse shift in investment should lead to lower saving and investment and a decrease in all rates, safe and risky. An increase in risk or risk aversion, or a higher demand for liquidity, should lead to a decrease in the safe rate but an increase in risky or less liquid rates. This suggests looking at what has happened to saving/investment rates and to risk premia.

Figure 3.4 shows the evolution of the gross saving rate for the world as a whole, as well as for high income and upper middle income countries (roughly corresponding to emerging markets), since 1992.

The figure shows three important evolutions. First, there was an increase in the saving rate in middle income countries (reflecting largely the high Chinese saving rate) from 2000 to 2008, which led to a focus on China's reserve accumulation and talk of a "global savings glut" but was followed

---

12. For reference, see Rachel and Summers (2019, table 7), which yields the following conclusions. Non-policy shifts in factors affecting private saving and investment would have led, by themselves, to a decline in r^* of 6.9% in the "industrialized world" since 1970. Of these, the main factors are total factor productivity (TFP) growth (−1.8%), population growth (−0.6%), longer retirement (−1.1%), and inequality (−0.7%). These were, however, partly offset by policies, with the main factors being higher public debt (1.2%) and social security (1.2%), which by themselves would have led to an *increase* in r^* of 3.7%. The net result was a decrease in r^* of 6.9% −3.7%, thus 3.2%,

13. In an open economy, it may lead to a smaller increase in investment than in saving and thus a current account surplus. At the world level, saving has to be equal to investment.

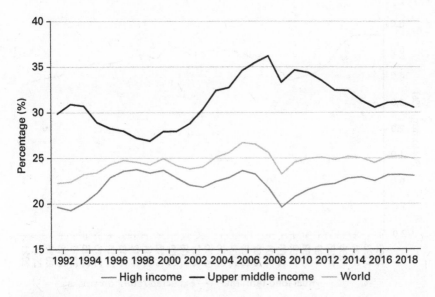

Figure 3.4
Gross saving rate: high income, upper middle income, and world.
Source: World Bank open data on gross savings.

by a decrease from then on. Second, the saving rate of high income countries was stable, except for a dip during the Great Financial Crisis. Third, as low income and lower middle income countries account for little of world saving, the result of the evolutions in high income and middle income countries is a fairly stable saving rate for the world as a whole. This suggests that, to the extent that there were positive saving shifts, they were accompanied by adverse investment shifts, both factors resulting in a roughly unchanged saving rate, but both factors contributing to a decrease in r^*.

Turning to risk and liquidity factors, the discussion above suggests looking at what has happened to safe versus risky rates. Thus, figure 3.5 shows, for the United States, the evolution of the safe real rate, measured as in figure 3.1, and a measure of the expected rate of return on holding the Standard and Poor's (S&P) 500 since 1992.[14] The expected rate of return on

---

14. Note the shift from moving from world saving and investment in figure 3.4 to a focus on the United States only. If it could be done, it would make sense to compare the world safe rate with the world expected rate of return on stocks. This is a much larger endeavor than anything I can do here.

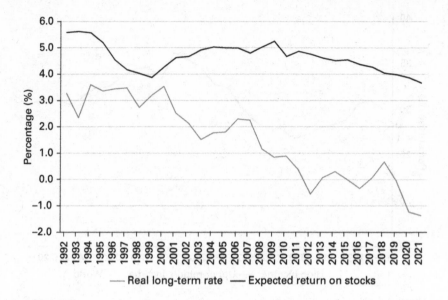

Figure 3.5
Safe real rate and expected real rate of return on equity.
Sources: The safe rate is constructed as the 10-year nominal rate minus 10-year forecast of inflation from the Survey of Professional Forecasters. The expected real rate of
return is constructed as the sum of the dividend-price ratio from Case and Shiller,
and the 10-year average output growth forecast from the Survey of Professional
Forecasters.

stocks is constructed using an extension of Gordon's formula, which states
that the expected rate of return can be expressed approximately as the sum
of the dividend price ratio plus a weighted average of the future growth rates
of dividends.[15] Given that there is no available time series for real-time forecasts of future dividends, I approximate them by forecasts of output growth
over the following 10 years, taking a simple unweighted average of forecast
US output growth over the 10 years.[16]

Figure 3.5 sends again a clear message. It shows that the expected rate of
return on stocks has decreased, but much less than the real rate of return

---

15. More specifically, the expected rate of return, $R(t)$, is given by $R(t) \approx ((R-g)/(1+R)) \sum_{i=1}^{i=\infty} ((1+g)/(1+r))^i Eg(t+1)$, where R and g are the average rate of return
and the average growth rate and $Eg(t+i)$ is the forecast of growth in year $t+i$. For a
derivation, see Blanchard 1993.
16. The focus on US growth is not quite right, as 30% of the revenues of S&P 500
companies come from abroad. I have not tried to improve the measure.

on bonds (about 2% over the period, compared to 4% for the safe rate). The difference between the two (i.e., the equity premium), has substantially increased.[17] This suggests that part of the decrease in the real safe rate reflects a higher demand for safety or/and a higher demand for liquidity on the part of financial investors.[18] More has been at work than just shifts in saving and investment.

Before moving to conclusions and potential implications for fiscal policy, I want to take up two issues—namely, the relation between interest rates and growth rates and the role of demographics in the determination of r^*. The reason is that I find some of the discussion of the first misleading and discussion of the second confusing.

3.2 Interest Rates and Growth Rates

There is a widely shared belief that the decrease in interest rates reflects in large part a decrease in growth rates. Indeed, a large part of the research on the causes of low interest rates starts from a theoretical relation between interest rates and growth, known as the Euler equation. Its logic is straightforward.[19]

Ignoring uncertainty, standard utility maximization suggests that individuals form consumption plans according to the following relation:

$$g_c = \sigma(r - \theta),$$

where g_c is the rate of growth of individual consumption, σ is the elasticity of substitution between consumption across time, and θ is the individual's subjective discount rate. The relation, which is known as the *Euler equation*, is intuitive. Suppose that the interest rate is equal to the subjective discount rate, so $r - \theta = 0$. In this case, $g_c = 0$, and people will want to plan so as to

---

17. Put another way, and in the light of high stock valuations and questions about whether we are observing a bubble, if the equity premium had remained constant, stock prices would be substantially *higher* than they are today. Conclusions are very similar if one uses the earnings-price ratio as a proxy for the expected rate of return.

18. A similar point is made by Farhi and Gourio 2019.

19. This section is aimed at discussing a particular direction of research (and deals with an old gripe of mine), but it can be skipped without harm. Its conclusion is that, while the growth rate may well affect saving and investment, there is no tight relation between growth rates and interest rates, either on theoretical or empirical grounds.

have flat consumption over their life. If $r > \theta$, then it becomes attractive to defer consumption and to plan on an increasing consumption path, so $g_c > 0$. How much to twist the path in response to the interest rate depends on the elasticity of substitution σ. If it is low, people are not willing to trade off consumption much across periods, and the effect of $(r - \theta)$ on the slope of the path is small. If it is high, the effect is larger.

Assuming that this holds, at least approximately, for an individual, what does this imply about aggregate consumption? If all people are identical and live forever, what holds for one individual holds in the aggregate and thus holds for the economy as a whole. If the economy is in approximate steady state, the growth rate of consumption is equal to the growth of output, which is itself equal to the growth rate of potential output. The interest rate must then be able to induce consumers to choose a consumption path consistent with the growth rate of potential output. So we can invert the relation above to get a causal relation from output growth to the interest rate:

$$r = \theta + g/\sigma,$$

where g is the growth rate of potential output.

This suggests a tight relation between the interest rate and the growth rate. For example, a slowdown in productivity growth, which decreases the growth rate of potential output, leads to a decrease in the interest rate, with an effect that depends on the size of σ.[20] This has led various researchers to use this equation (or a generalization of it to allow for richer specifications of utility and for uncertainty) to organize their examination of the data.

Where does this approach go wrong? One may argue that standard utility maximization does not describe individual decisions accurately, and there is plenty of evidence that this is indeed the case. But the main issue is elsewhere. The actual economy is composed of finitely lived individuals. Even if each of us were to plan consumption according to an Euler equation and decided, for example, to have an upward-sloping consumption path (if $r > \theta$), this has no implication at all for the relation between the

---

20. A particularly nerdy footnote: This might lead, if σ is large enough, to $r < g$. In this case, however, households can achieve infinite utility, and this case is typically excluded a priori in this class of models. David Romer (2012, 51) further discusses this issue.

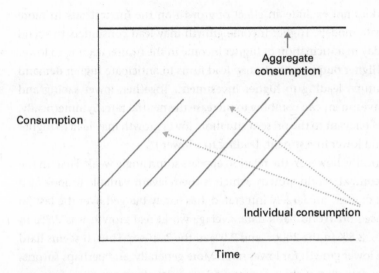

Figure 3.6
Individual and aggregate consumption

interest rate and the aggregate growth rate. This is shown very simply in figure 3.6.

Assume people live for two periods (think 30 years for each period). The same number of people are born each period.[21] There is no population growth, nor technological progress, so all individuals face the same budget constraint when they are born and choose the same consumption path. If $r > \theta$, they all choose an upward-sloping path, so each individual consumption path slopes up. But aggregate consumption, which in each period is the sum of the consumption of the young and the consumption of the old, is obviously flat, whatever the slope of individual paths, thus whatever value of the interest rate.

In other words, if people have finite lives (which they do), *no matter how long they live*, there is no reason to expect the Euler relation to hold for aggregate consumption.[22]

---

21. This model, with its very simple population structure, is known as the basic overlapping generation model (OLG). Despite being extremely stylized, it helps clarify arguments and will prove very useful at various points in the book.

22. As is well known, Barro (1974) argued that even if people have finite lives, they may care about their children, and their children may care about their own children, and so on, so that through those links, people may have in effect infinite horizons.

This does not exclude an effect of growth on the interest rate in more appropriate models. Higher income growth may lead consumers to spend more today in anticipation of higher income in the future, leading to lower saving. Higher output growth may lead firms to anticipate higher demand in the future, leading to higher investment. Together, lower saving and higher investment can combine to increase the neutral rate. Symmetrically, and more relevant to the present situation, lower growth may lead to higher saving and lower investment, leading to a lower r^*.

Empirically, however, the relation appears surprisingly weak. First, in the current context, world growth, which is the relevant variable to look at if financial markets are largely integrated, has barely budged over the last 30 years. Based on World Bank data, average world real growth was 2.7% in the 1990s, 2.8% in the 2000s, and 2.9% in the 2010s.[23] Thus, it seems hard to blame lower growth for lower rates. More generally, and perhaps surprisingly, the data do not show a strong relation (let alone causality) between growth rates and interest rates. For example, using the long Schmelzing sample, and seven-year centered moving averages, the correlation is actually strongly negative (Schmelzing 2018, fig. 16) and is unstable across major historical episodes. Similarly, Borio, Disyatat, and Rungcharoenkitkul (2019, table 1), looking at correlations since the beginning of the twentieth century, show the correlation to be slightly negative and unstable across time.

With respect to the underlying long-term evolutions, I suspect that the *level* of output rather than its growth rate may be the more relevant variable, as argued, for example, by Von Weizsacker and Kramer (2021). Poor people hardly save because their income is just enough to sustain their consumption. The same is true of poor countries. As people become richer and as countries become richer, saving increases, leading to a decrease in the neutral interest rate. Indeed, based on World Bank data, the saving rate in low income countries is much lower than in richer countries, averaging 12%

The conditions for this to be true are stringent and unlikely to be satisfied. I find the overlapping generation model a better model to work with than the infinite horizon consumer model.

23. Note that when we look at debt dynamics in a given country, the relevant growth rate g is the country growth rate. When looking at the determination of r^*, and assuming integrated financial markets, the relevant growth rate is the world growth rate.

from 1994 to 2007 (the period for which the data exist) compared to about 25% for the world as a whole.[24]

3.3 The Role of Demographics

Can demographic evolutions explain some of the decrease in the interest rate? The literature is confusing. Some argue that demographic evolutions have indeed led to a decrease in r^*, but they will lead in the future to a major decrease in saving and thus a higher r^* (Goodhart and Pradhan 2020). Others argue the opposite and forecast further declines in the interest rate (Auclert et al. 2021). Yet others (Platzer and Peruffo 2021) conclude that demographics explain much of the decrease in r^*, but looking forward, they forecast r^* to be about flat from now on.[25]

There are three major demographic evolutions at play around the world:

• The first is the decrease in fertility rates (the average number of children per woman), which is more pronounced in emerging markets and developing economies but present nearly everywhere. The global fertility rate has decreased from 5 in 1950 to 2.5 today; looking forward, it is expected to decrease further, but at a much lower pace, reaching 2.3 in the 2045–2050 forecast period.[26]

• The second is the increase in life expectancy, which again has happened everywhere. Global life expectancy has increased from 45 years in 1950 to 72 years today. Forecasts are that this will continue at roughly the same pace in the future, except in very rich countries, where the increase will be more limited.[27]

• The third, which was most pronounced in advanced economies, is what is known as the "baby boom," a major but temporary bump in births after

24. This is clearly not true of all countries all the time—consider the rise of the saving rate in China at a still low level of income per capita.
25. See also Favero, Gozluklu, and Tamoni 2011.
26. United Nations, "World population by level of fertility over time (1950–2100)," *Our World in Data*, 2012, https://ourworldindata.org/uploads/2014/02/World-population-by-level-of-fertility.png.
27. United Nations, "Life expectancy, 2019," *Our World in Data*, 2019, https://ourworldindata.org/grapher/life-expectancy?time=1770..2019&country=Africa+Americas+Asia+Europe+Oceania+OWID_WRL.

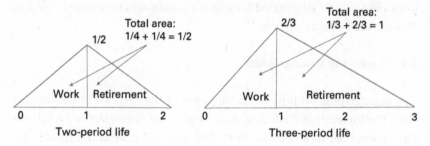

Figure 3.7
Life expectancy and total wealth

World War II. As baby boomers age, the effect of this bump will fade over time.

To think about the effects of each of these three factors, I will use a simple diagram (figure 3.7), based again on a simple overlapping generation structure.

Suppose that people live for two periods, working during the first and receiving an income of 1, retiring in the second and thus consuming out of their saving; suppose, too, that the interest rate and the discount rate are both equal to zero, so people want flat consumption paths. The diagram on the left of figure 3.7 shows the evolution of the wealth for one consumer throughout that person's life: Wealth increases from 0 to 1/2 at retirement age, and then declines from 1/2 back to zero during retirement. Assuming that population is constant, the cross-section of wealth is also shown in figure 3.7, and total wealth in the economy is given by the area of the triangle, thus $1/4 + 1/4 = 1/2$.

Now suppose that there is an increase in longevity and that people live for three periods, again working in the first and receiving an income of 1, but now being retired for two periods. The diagram on the right of figure 3.7 shows the evolution of wealth for one consumer throughout that person's life. To keep consumption constant throughout life, consumers now need to save 2/3 of their income when working. Wealth increases from 0 to 2/3 at retirement age, and then declines back to zero over the two retirement periods. Looking at the new steady state, assuming that population is constant, total assets in the economy are given by the area of the triangle, thus $1/3 + 2/3 = 1$, thus twice as much as before.

The assumptions underlying the figure are simplistic, and the change in life expectancy is obviously too extreme. The dynamic adjustment that takes place when longevity increases is ignored. The age of retirement is assumed fixed; if it increased in proportion to the increase in life—namely, by 1/2—the saving rate would remain constant (historically, the retirement age has increased less than proportionately). The presence of pay-as-you-go social security reduces the effect on saving. People save for reasons other than life-cycle considerations. People leave bequests. But the basic conclusion is robust, and it is a clear and important one: Longer life expectancy is likely to lead to an increase in saving and thus a decrease in the interest rate.[28]

Similar exercises can be done to think about the effects of lower fertility and of the baby boom. I leave computations to the reader, who can use the same diagrammatic approach. A lower proportion of workers relative to retirees decreases overall saving but decreases income by proportionately more, so the saving rate (which is the ratio of the two) again goes up. The baby boom leads to an increase in the saving rate when the boomers work and a decrease in the saving rate when they retire, an effect that is relevant today but will fade in the future. The dominant factor, however, looking forward, will be longer life expectancy, and this suggests continuing downward pressure on the interest rate.

3.4 Conclusions

What about the future?

Investors appear confident that interest rates will remain low for some time. This can be inferred from deriving risk neutral probabilities from option prices on Treasury bonds of different maturities. The results, as of the time of writing (January 2022), for the United States, are shown in table 3.1.

Investors give, for example, a probability of 12% to the short US nominal interest rate exceeding 4% in five years, a probability of 16% to it exceeding 4% in 10 years. The corresponding probabilities are 4% and 8% for the euro zone, and 7% and 10% for the United Kingdom. Probabilities that the

---

28. It is sometimes said that longer life expectancy means a higher proportion of dissavers—a proposition that is correct—and thus lower overall saving (which is not). Figure 3.7 shows why this is the wrong way of thinking.

Table 3.1
Probabilities that nominal interest rates will be less than a given value in 5 or 10 years, as of January 2022.

Currency	Expiration	< 0%	< 1%	< 2%	< 3%	< 4%
USD	5y	11%	27%	54%	77%	88%
USD	10y	16%	29%	50%	71%	84%
EUR	5y	50%	76%	88%	93%	96%
EUR	10y	38%	60%	77%	86%	92%
UK	5y	25%	51%	74%	87%	93%
UK	10y	32%	52%	70%	83%	90%

Source: Private communication.

nominal rate exceeds 4% are particularly interesting, as this is a plausible forecast of what nominal gross domestic product (GDP) growth may be over the next 5 to 10 years (2% real and 2% inflation).[29]

Are they right? I believe they roughly are, both about the fact that the probability is high that long safe interest rates remain lower than growth rates for a decade or more, and about the fact that the probability is, however, less than one.

I read the steady decline in rates as evidence of deep underlying factors at work: Real interest rates have steadily declined in all major economies for more than three decades. This decline was not caused by the Global Financial Crisis or the Covid crisis. In most advanced economies, 10-year real rates are now typically 3% lower than 10-year real growth forecasts.

Large negative values of $(r - g)$ have happened in the past, and the sign of $(r - g)$ eventually and sometimes quickly and durably reversed. But these episodes were typically due to unexpected inflation, financial repression, or r being less than r^*. This is not the case today. If anything, the fact that the ELB is binding in many countries indicates that the opposite is true—that r^* is less than r.

I wish we had a better sense of exactly which factors have contributed to the decline. The list of suspects is long, but their individual role is not well established. My reading of the evidence leads me to put more weight on shifts in saving, due to demographics and to higher income, and on

29. In assessing $r - g$, one can use real interest rates (using, however, the GDP deflator rather than the CPI) and real growth rates, or nominal interest rates and nominal growth rates, as I do here.

increases in the demand for liquid and safe assets. In general, looking at the longer list of potential factors, I see no obvious reason why their effect should change sign any time soon.

Some may, however. Of the non-policy factors, there is a nonnegligible probability of a pickup in the rate of technological progress, associated with green investment, for example. This might lead to higher growth (although the effect may be more on the nature of growth than the rate of growth) and thus even more negative $r^* - g$. But it would also lead to a large increase in investment. Estimates are that green investment might increase overall investment by 2% of GDP for a decade or more. This would lead to sustained higher aggregate demand and thus an increase in r^*.[30,31]

And, coming back to the main theme of the book, the main policy factor—fiscal policy—is likely to matter very much:

• A sharp temporary increase in public spending may lead for some time to a sharp increase in r^*, forcing central banks to increase r to avoid overheating. At the time of writing, there is indeed a serious worry that the Biden stimulus of 2021 may indeed lead to overheating, increasing inflation, and the need for the Fed to increase rates substantially.[32] The effect should, however, eventually disappear as the effects of the stimulus on demand fade over time.

• Pushing the argument further, a sustained sequence of large deficits could increase debt ratios and, by implication, increase r^* permanently, increasing $r^* - g$ and even possibly changing the sign of the inequality. Estimates of the effect of debt on the neutral rate in the literature (which are unfortunately not much better than back-of-the-envelope computations; more on this topic in chapter 5) suggest that a 1% increase in the debt ratio leads to an increase in the neutral interest rate of 2 to 4 basis points. Thus, were public debt ratios (worldwide) to increase to 50% of GDP, say, this might lead to an increase in $r^* - g$ of 1% to 2%, substantially narrowing the difference

---

30. The International Energy Agency (2021) estimates that a global transition to net zero by 2050 would imply increasing global investment in energy from 2.5% of world GDP in the 2016–2020 period to 4.5% by 2030, after which it would gradually decline to return to 2.5% by 2050.

31. For a contrary and more pessimistic view of the future of technological progress, see Gordon 2016. For a more optimistic view, see Brynjolfsson and McAfee 2014.

32. I shall come back to a discussion of US fiscal policy and its implications in chapter 6.

between r^* and g. Such a debt outcome is unlikely, but the computation makes the point that the more fiscal policy is used, the higher r^* will be relative to g.

• Indeed, one of the main conclusions of this book will be that the goal of fiscal policy should be to maintain r^* high enough that the ELB condition is not strictly binding and could be possibly higher. If such a fiscal policy is implemented, this would put a floor on how low r^* can be.

4 Debt Sustainability

With the ground having been prepared, the remaining chapters turn to the implications of low interest rates for fiscal policy. There are two separate questions to be answered, which are sometimes mixed up:

• How much "fiscal space" does a country have? Or more precisely, how much room does the country have to increase its debt until this raises issues of debt sustainability?

• How should this fiscal space be used? The fact that there is space does not mean that it should be used. Fiscal policy is about whether, when, and how to use that space.

This chapter is about the first question. It has seven sections.

Section 4.1 starts with the arithmetic of debt dynamics *under certainty*, focusing on the role of $(r - g)$. It shows the respective roles of $(r - g)$, debt, and primary balances. It shows some of the dramatic implications of $(r - g < 0)$: Governments can run primary deficits and keep their debt ratios stable. Formally, there is no issue of debt sustainability. Whatever primary deficits governments run, debt may increase but it will not explode. Put another way, governments appear to have infinite fiscal space...

However, this conclusion is too strong, for two reasons. First, fiscal policy, in the form of higher debt or deficits, increases aggregate demand, and thus increases the neutral rate r^*. To the extent that the monetary authority adjusts the actual rate r in response to r^*, this increases $(r - g)$ and thus reduces fiscal space. Second, uncertainty is of the essence. Debt sustainability is fundamentally a probabilistic concept. A tentative operational definition might go as follows: Debt is sustainable if the probability of a debt explosion is small (one still must define "explosion" and "small," which can be done). With this in mind, section 4.2 discusses the various sources of uncertainty and their potential effects on debt sustainability. It explains the respective roles of the debt ratio, the maturity of the debt, the distribution of current and future primary balances, and the distribution of current and future $(r-g)$. It shows how stochastic debt sustainability analysis (SDSA) can be used by governments, investors, and rating agencies. It shows how realistic reductions in debt from current levels have little effect on the probability that debt is sustainable; in contrast, it shows the importance of contingent plans in case $(r-g)$ increases and reverses sign.

Section 4.3 looks at the case for fiscal rules to ensure debt sustainability. SDSAs can only be done in situ, for each year, for each country. The assumptions they require about the future evolution of $(r-g)$, for example, leave room for disagreement. Can one design second-best, more mechanistic rules as guardrails and still leave enough room for fiscal policy to perform its macroeconomic role? This is the question currently under discussion in the European Union. I express skepticism that a mechanistic rule can work well, but if a rule is nevertheless going to be adopted, I suggest the direction it should explore. I argue that the analysis in section 4.2 suggests a rule that adjusts the primary balance in response to debt service—rather than debt—over time.

Section 4.4 discusses the relation between public investment and debt sustainability. For political reasons, fiscal austerity has often led to a decrease in public investment rather than in other forms of spending. The transparency case for separating the current account and the capital account (known as "capital budgeting") is a strong one. The case for full debt financing of public investment, which is sometimes made, is weaker: To the extent that public investment generates direct financial returns to the government, it can indeed be at least partially financed by debt without affecting debt sustainability. One may also argue that, by increasing growth, it increases future fiscal revenues. But much of public investment, even if it increases social welfare, does not generate financial returns for the state and has uncertain effects on growth. Thus, it can affect debt sustainability, and this must be taken into account in the way it is financed. Section 4.4 shows how this can be integrated in an analysis of debt sustainability.

Section 4.5 looks at the risk of sudden stops and the potential role of central banks in this context. Sovereign debt markets (and many other markets as well) are subject to sudden stops in which investors either drop out or ask for large spreads even in the absence of large changes in fundamentals. This has been more of an issue in emerging economies' markets, but as the European debt crisis has shown, it is also relevant for advanced economies. Even if fundamentals suggest little debt sustainability risk and justify low rates, another equilibrium may arise where investors worry and ask for a spread over safe rates, increasing debt service and increasing the probability that debt is unsustainable, justifying their worries in the first place. Given the nature of this kind of equilibrium it is often referred to as "sunspot equilibrium." I argue that the issue is relevant, but that it takes extremely low levels of debt to eliminate the scope for multiple equilibria, levels far below current debt levels. Realistic reductions of debt over the next decades will not eliminate this risk.

I then look at whether central banks can reduce or even eliminate this risk. I distinguish between two sources for the increase in spreads: sunspots or deteriorations in fundamentals. Central banks, I argue, by being large stable investors, can prevent multiple equilibria and eliminate spreads that are due to sunspots, but the conclusion is less obvious when spreads are due, at least in part, to deteriorated fundamentals. The reason, in short, is that central banks are parts of the consolidated government, and their interventions change the composition but not the size of the overall consolidated government liabilities, nor the overall risk. I discuss why this may be different in the case of the European Central Bank and in its ability to decrease Italian spreads during the Covid crisis.

Section 4.6 takes up two issues that have come up about the relation of central banks to debt sustainability. Some observers have argued that, through quantitative easing (QE) and large-scale purchases of government bonds, central banks are monetizing the deficits and bailing out governments. I argue that this is simply not the case. Others have argued that, to alleviate the debt burden, central banks should simply write off the government bonds they hold on their balance sheet. I argue that it is not needed, and if it were to be done, it would do nothing to improve the budget constraint of the government.

In the concluding section 4.7, I note that negative $(r - g)$ makes the dynamics of debt much more benign. This does not make the issue of debt sustainability disappear, however, both because of endogeneity and the effect of fiscal policy back on the neutral interest rate and because of uncertainty, in particular with respect to r.

The best way to assess debt sustainability is through the use of SDSAs, an approach that takes into account the specificities of each country and each year. Given the complexity of the assessment, I am skeptical that one can rely on quantitative rules. If, however, such rules are used, they should be based on requiring the primary surplus to adjust to debt service, defined as $((r-g)/(1+g))b(-1)$, rather to debt itself. Exceptions cannot be avoided, however, such as the need to allow for larger primary deficits when the central bank is constrained by the effective lower bound (ELB).

4.1   The Surprising Debt Dynamics When $(r-g) < 0$

The dynamics of public debt are given by the following relation:

$$B = (1+r)B(-1) - S, \text{ or equivalently } B - B(-1) = rB(-1) - S.$$

Here, B is the real value of end-of-period debt, $B(-1)$ is its lagged value (think of the time interval as, say, one year), r is the real interest rate on debt, and S is the real value of the primary balance, defined as taxes minus non-interest spending (the mnemonic S stands for surplus: other things being equal, a positive primary balance—a positive value of S—decreases debt).[1,2]

---

1. The overall deficit is given by $(rB(-1) - S)$. In official reports and in the press, however, the deficit is typically reported as $(iB(-1) - S)$ and is thus an incorrect measure of the increase in the real value of debt. It needs to be corrected there is a difference between the nominal and the real interest rate (in this case, the realized ex post real interest rate, $i - \pi$, rather than the ex ante rate, $i - \pi^e$), a difference that is, by definition, equal to inflation. This correction matters—and it used to matter much more when inflation was high. With debt equal to, say, 100% of GDP, and inflation at 2%, the correct measure of the deficit is 2% lower (better) than the official measure. When, in the 1970s, inflation was close to 10% and the debt ratio was 50%, the difference was equal to 5% of GDP, a very substantial difference.

2. An anecdote: In 1981, Ronald Reagan announced that deficits were getting out of hand (at the time, an official deficit of $59.5 billion for fiscal year 1980 ... those were the days), and that this justified major cuts in spending. Jeffrey Sachs and I then wrote an op-ed for the *New York Times* (March 6, 1981) arguing that while nominal rates were a high 12%, inflation also ran at 10% (so real rates were only 2%, and high nominal rates reflected high inflation), and that once the correction for inflation was made, the correctly measured deficit was only $14 billion, less than 0.5% of gross national product (GNP). Our op-ed triggered a response published on March 13 by the *New York Times*, by a famous Harvard alumnus, who accused us of being inflation lovers and recommended that Harvard not to give us tenure.

What matters in a growing economy is not debt, however, but rather the ratio of debt to gross domestic product (GDP), the "debt ratio" for short.[3] Define the growth rate of output g so that $(1+g) \equiv Y/Y(-1)$, then divide both sides of the equation above by Y to get

$$b = \frac{(1+r)}{(1+g)} b(-1) - s,$$

where $b \equiv B/Y$ is the debt ratio and $s \equiv S/Y$ is the ratio of the primary balance to GDP. Reorganize to get:

$$b - b(-1) = \frac{(r-g)}{(1+g)} b(-1) - s. \tag{4.1}$$

This is the fundamental equation for debt dynamics. The change in the debt ratio depends on two terms: the primary balance ratio and the product of the (lagged) debt ratio and $(r-g)$. Why $(r-g)$? For the reason given in chapter 1: Assuming a zero-primary balance, debt increases at rate r, output increases at rate g, so the debt ratio increases at $(r-g)$—note that the term in $(1+g)$ must be there but is inessential to the discussion. As g is a small number, $(1+g)$ is very close to one.[4]

The standard discussion of debt dynamics has typically assumed that $(r-g)$ was positive. This implies that, to stabilize the debt ratio, the government must run a primary surplus. To see that, put $b = b(-1)$ in equation (4.1). The required primary balance is then given by

$$s = \frac{(r-g)}{(1+g)} b. \tag{4.2}$$

The larger the debt (let me forget the "ratio" part in places, to make the writing lighter), the larger the required surplus. So, if the government runs deficits and increases debt, then sooner or later, in order to stabilize debt, it will have to generate a larger primary surplus, either through an increase in taxes or a decrease in spending or both. If it does not, then debt will explode over time.

---

3. One may question the use of GDP in the denominator. For thinking about debt sustainability, a better ratio might be the ratio of debt to fiscal revenues. (The ratio of fiscal revenues to GDP for advanced economies has remained fairly stable since 2000, around 35%, so looking at the evolution of the ratio of debt to revenues rather than the ratio of debt to GDP would have roughly the same implications.) For other purposes, for example, for thinking about the effect on debt on the investment rate (the ratio of investment to GDP), then the ratio of debt to GDP is more appropriate.
4. Had I written the debt dynamics in continuous time, the term would not be there.

Now suppose, as is currently the case, that $(r-g) < 0$. Then, to stabilize the debt ratio, the required primary balance is still given by equation (4.2). But now, given that $(r-g) < 0$, the government does not need to run a primary surplus. Instead, it can run a primary deficit. Indeed, the larger the debt ratio, the larger the primary deficit it can run while keeping the debt ratio stable!

This last result seems paradoxical. The way to understand it is as follows. The government must pay interest r on the debt, thus leading to interest payments equal to rb. But, because output increases at rate g over time, it can issue new debt every year in amount gb and still keep the debt ratio constant. If g exceeds r, then the revenues from new issues are larger than the interest payments, and the higher the debt, the larger is the difference between the two.[5]

The implications of equation (4.2) can be stated in even more striking ways:

• Suppose that starting again from a stable debt ratio, the government further increases the primary deficit permanently by some amount. Then, from equation (4.1), the debt ratio will increase. But it will not explode, converging instead to a value of $s(1+g)/(r-g)$ (inverting equation (4.2) to think of b as a function of s). Thus, if we think of debt sustainability as the statement that debt will not explode, then under the assumption that $(r-g) < 0$, then debt is always sustainable. It may increase, but it will eventually converge rather than explode. Put in terms of "fiscal space," governments have infinite fiscal space.

The notion that debt cannot explode may, however, be more convincing theoretically than empirically. If $(r-g)$ is close to zero, and if the government runs a large primary deficit, debt may increase for a long time and converge to a very high level. For example, if $s = -3\%$, $g = 2\%$, and $r = 1\%$, so $(r-g) = -1\%$, debt will still converge, but to a high 306% of GDP. In

---

5. Because the outcome depends on the state issuing new debt every period, the outcome has been called a Ponzi game, or Ponzi finance, by some researchers. I think this is misleading. Ponzi schemes indeed depend on the ability of the Ponzi issuer to attract new investors every period in order to pay the interest due to existing investors, but typically the rate at which the number of potential investors must increase to sustain the scheme largely exceeds the rate of increase of the available investors' pool; eventually, the scheme is no longer viable and collapses. In the case of the government, if $r < g$ remains true forever (a big if, as I discuss below), there are potentially sufficiently new investors to sustain the scheme forever.

practice, such a large increase may be impossible to distinguish from an actual explosion. I shall return to this later.

• Suppose that, initially, the debt ratio and the primary balance satisfy equation (4.2), so the debt ratio is stable. Now suppose the government runs a larger primary deficit for one year—say, by reducing taxes for one year. It then returns to the same primary balance thereafter. The debt ratio will initially increase, but over time, it will return to its initial level.[6] In other words, the government can issue debt and never raise taxes to pay for the additional debt!

These are striking results, and they force us to question the standard discussion of debt (along the lines of asking whether "our children will have to pay for the debt through higher taxes").[7]

And the implications of $(r-g) < 0$ can be seen in the data: For example, despite the worries about the high levels of debt and the large primary

---

6. The basic algebra is as follows: Call b^* the initial level of debt and $s^* = (r-g)/(1+g)\, b^*$ the associated initial primary balance. Then, if after the one-time decrease in taxes s goes back to its initial value s^*, one can rewrite equation (4.1) as $(b - b^*) - (b(-1) - b^*) = ((r-g)/(1+g))(b(-1) - b^*)$. The limit, as we look further and further out, is $b = b^*$.

7. Yet another way of stating the implications of equation (4.1) when $r < g$ has been explored by Ricardo Reis (2020, 2022). Assume r and g to be constant and future surpluses to be known with certainty (these assumptions are not needed, but they simplify the exposition). When $r > g$, integrating the debt dynamics equation forward, and assuming that the debt ratio does not eventually explode, implies that the ratio of debt to GDP must be equal to the present discounted value of the ratios of primary surpluses to output, discounted at rate $r - g$. This relation plays a central role in many theories—for example, in the fiscal theory of the price level developed by John Cochrane (2022). When $r - g < 0$, however, the discount factor associated with future surpluses increases with time, and the present discounted value of future surpluses becomes infinite. In that case, Reis proposes to rewrite the equation for debt dynamics by adding and subtracting $\hat{r}b(t-1)$, where $\hat{r}$ is a discount rate larger than the growth rate (e.g., the average marginal product of capital, which we saw in the previous chapter is higher than the growth rate), so $\hat{r} > g$. This gives the following equation (ignoring the $(1+g)$ term for simplicity):

$$b(t) = (1 + r - g)b(t-1) - s(t) + \hat{r}b(t-1) - \hat{r}b(t-1),$$

or equivalently,

$$b(t) = (1 + \hat{r} - g)b(t-1) - s(t) - (\hat{r} - r)b(t-1).$$

For any choice of $\hat{r}$ variable that is greater than g, we can again integrate forward and, assuming that the discounted value of the debt ratio does not explode, obtain

deficits, the International Monetary Fund (IMF) forecasts that 18 out of 27 advanced economies will have decreasing debt ratios by 2026, with debt ratios increasing by slightly more than 2 percentage points in only three countries, Belgium, South Korea, and the United States.[8]

In short, debt dynamics are much more favorable when $(r - g) < 0$. But taking the results above at face value would be wrong for two reasons, which will parallel the warnings made in chapter 3 about the course of interest rates in the future:

- *Endogeneity*. The interest rate depends, in part, on fiscal policy. Sustained large deficits, either domestically or globally (with the relative weights of the two depending on the degree of integration of financial markets), are likely to increase the neutral rate r^* and, by implication, the actual rate r, making debt dynamics less attractive. I argued in chapter 3 that a durable sign reversal of $(r - g)$ was unlikely for a long time to come, but if it happened, debt dynamics would become much worse and governments would have to run primary surpluses in order to stabilize the debt.

- *Uncertainty*. Even if the mean forecasts of $(r - g) < 0$ are negative over a long horizon, these forecasts come with substantial uncertainty (although not necessarily more now than in earlier times). The next step is thus to

---

debt as the present value of two terms:

$$b(t) = \sum_{1}^{\infty} (1 + \hat{r} - g)^{-i} s(t+i) + \sum_{1}^{\infty} (1 + \hat{r} - g)^{-i} (\hat{r} - r) b(t+i-1).$$

In words, debt can be expressed as the present discounted value of primary surpluses, discounted at rate $(\hat{r} - g)$ plus what Reis calls a debt revenue term, the present discounted value of the difference between $\hat{r} - r$ times debt. He then goes on to think about what determines this revenue term and presents alternative models, where liquidity or idiosyncratic risk determine the difference between the safe rate r and $\hat{r}$ taken to be the marginal product of capital. Ricardo and I have had fun discussions, but we have agreed to disagree. I do not see what is gained conceptually by that step. Clearly, the debt dynamics are the same whether one uses the original equation or the modified equation. I do not see on what grounds one chooses $\hat{r}$: Why not the rate on junk bonds, which would make the present value of surpluses smaller and the debt revenue bigger? To the extent that debt is safe, the appropriate discount rate is the safe rate, not any other. And while what is behind the difference between the safe rate and the average marginal product of capital is very important from a welfare viewpoint, I do not see what is gained by thinking in terms of the debt revenue term.

8. IMF Fiscal Monitor, April 2021, table A8.

think about debt dynamics, debt sustainability, and fiscal space, taking uncertainty into account.

4.2 Uncertainty, Sustainability, and Fiscal Space

Take into account uncertainty, and go back to equation (4.1). The evolution of debt over time depends on current and future realizations of $(r - g)$ and s. Unless we are willing to put an upper bound on the distribution of $(r - g)$, the probability that debt explodes may be very small, but it is not zero.[9] This suggests the following operational definition of debt sustainability: "Debt is sustainable if the probability is small that debt is on an exploding trajectory n years out."

This makes it clear that sustainability is a probabilistic statement. This clearly does not settle it, as one has to decide what an "exploding trajectory" is, what n should be, and what "small enough" actually means. But it suggests doing the following exercise, known as a stochastic debt sustainability analysis, or SDSA:

• Compute the distribution of debt over the next n years, based not just on the mean forecasts but also on assumed distributions of $(r - g)$ and s around these forecasts.

• Choose n by assessing the trade-off between the quality of the forecasts— which deteriorates sharply for large values of n, say, more than 10 years— and the need to allow for nonexplosive movements in debt. An increase in the debt ratio for a few years is not worrisome and does not necessarily threaten debt sustainability.[10]

---

9. Put another way, if there is a positive probability that $r - g$ is positive and that the primary balance can show a deficit ($s < 0$), then there is a positive probability that debt will explode.

10. I am sweeping under the rug a difficult issue: the usefulness of very long horizon budget forecasts—say, over 30 years or more. These can show very high debt levels, but they depend strongly on assumptions we have little knowledge about. For example, Congressional Budget Office (CBO) forecasts of debt over the next 30 years (www.cbo.gov/data/budget-economic-data#1, March 2021) show a large increase in the debt ratio, from 102.3% in 2021 to 202.2% in 2051, rapidly exploding at the end of the sample. These forecast are, however, based on a nominal interest rate that increases to above 4% over time. Under the alternative assumption that the nominal rate will be 2% on average over the period, the debt ratio is "only" 140% in 2051 and close to stable by the end of the horizon. My tentative conclusion is not that one

• Choose an operational definition of "explosion." This may be, for example, a positive slope for the trajectory in the debt ratio as the horizon gets to n. So, following on the earlier discussion, making a distinction between rapid convergence to a high debt level and a strict debt explosion may be impossible to do in practice.

What the government will do if debt appears to be on an exploding path is clearly central to the assessment. Thus, it is useful to think of the exercise as proceeding in two steps.

• The first step is to do the exercise above under *existing* policies.[11] If these policies lead, with high probability, to a nonexploding debt ratio as the horizon gets to n, there is no need for the second step. If, however, existing and announced policies lead to an exploding debt ratio with high enough probability, then a second step is needed.

• The second step depends on who does it. If it is the government doing the exercise, then it needs to announce how it intends to modify existing or announced policies. If there is a fiscal agency or a fiscal council in place, its role may be to ask or even require the government to present a credible adjustment plan so that debt appears sustainable.[12] If it is an outside observer—say, an investment fund or a rating agency doing the exercise—then it has to assess the government's plan and determine whether, how, and when the government will actually adjust, whether it is likely to succeed, and thus whether debt is then sustainable or not.

The first and second steps are quite different in nature and require different types of information.

Formally, the first step requires assumptions about the joint distribution of $r, g,$ and s.

First moments—namely, mean forecasts for the three variables—are likely to be available from standard forecasting sources. The difficult task

---

should ignore the signal that there may be a fiscal problem further in the future, but that this discussion must be separate from the SDSA exercise.

11. There is some ambiguity about how to treat changes that are likely but have not yet been fully voted on. By law, the CBO must construct its baseline forecasts under "current law." In some cases, it is clear that aspects of the current law will be changed and programs that are supposed to expire will be extended, which sometimes leads to CBO baseline forecasts that are not truly forecasts.

12. CBO does not have the power to make such a request. It can, however, "score" the announced plan and let Congress decide.

is to make assumptions about the distributions. This is likely to require combining different sources of information: quantitative evidence on the covariations between the variables in the past in the form, for example, of vector autoregressions; macro model stochastic simulations to take into account the effects of policies and other shocks on output and government revenues; market information when available, such as the probability distributions for the US nominal rate that we saw at the end of chapter 3; and specific information about the future, such as information about implicit liabilities and the likelihood that the public retirement system will need to be partly financed from the general budget.

To the extent that uncertainty in r may be the most important issue at this juncture, the average maturity of the debt matters very much: A longer maturity of debt protects the government from a temporary increase in the short run interest rate, and it gives it more time to adjust to a permanent increase.[13] The currency denomination of debt also matters very much as well. Because of exchange rate movements, debt in foreign currency is likely to imply a much wider distribution for the ex post interest rate and thus for end of horizon debt.

A difficult practical issue is how to take into account the effect of sustainability risk itself on the interest rate and resulting debt dynamics: If, under the assumption that the country is able to borrow at the safe rate (or at the safe rate plus a fixed, say, historically given, risk premium), the SDSA shows a nonnegligible positive probability of a debt explosion. This implies that if the investors have access to the same information, they will ask for a risk premium and a higher rate. This higher rate in turn will lead to worse debt dynamics, leading to a higher probability of a debt explosion and in turn a higher risk premium, and so on. The nonlinearity makes solving for the endogenous risk premium and the equilibrium distribution of debt more difficult. In my ongoing work with Gonzalo Huertas and Michael Kister, we have made some progress (Blanchard, Kister, and Huertas 2021), but the work has convinced me of the difficulty of doing it in realistic SDSA settings. In practice, the best practical approach may be to first ignore the feedback effect and assume a fixed risk premium, but if the probability of explosion turns out to be nonnegligible, then redo the simulation by adding

---

13. For an interesting exercise, using the SDSA format to derive the implications and the optimal maturity composition of the debt for debt sustainability, see Zenios et al. 2021.

the spread implied by the probability of explosion to the initial path for the interest rate and iterate.

What do rating agencies actually do?

What do rating agencies do, and how much weight do they put on the level of debt in their ratings?[a]

A detailed description of the methodology used, for example, by S&P Global to determine its ratings, is given in Standard and Poor's 2019. The rating agency builds its ratings on five "pillars"; institutional (such as quality of governance, transparency, debt history), economic (income per capita, growth, volatility), external (currency status, external liquidity, external position), fiscal (debt ratio, debt service, performance, flexibility), and monetary (exchange rate regime, independence of the central bank, credibility).

Going from words to deeds: A literature review of the econometric determinants of ratings of sovereign debt shows that the explanatory variables that appear most often are GDP per capita, past default, the rate of inflation, debt, and deficits.[b]

To explore the role of debt itself, I started from a Goldman Sachs study (Ardagna 2018) that considered ratings from S&P Global, Moody's, and Fitch for 21 countries in the Organization for Economic Cooperation and Development (OECD) from 1984 to 2017 (subject to data availability for some countries). It mapped each of these ratings into 11 bins, from 1 to 11, with 11 being the best (AAA for all three rating agencies). It then ran an ordered probit for each of the three sets of ratings on a number of variables, the main ones being the log of real GDP per capita, the GDP growth rate, the unemployment rate, the inflation rate, the ratio of the current account balance to GDP, the ratio of the net international investment position to GDP, and two fiscal variables: the ratio of government debt to GDP and the ratio of the primary deficit to GDP. The most consistently significant variables were the log of real GDP per capita and the two fiscal variables, with t-statistics above 10 for the ratio of debt to GDP.

To assess the contribution of the ratio of debt to GDP, I replicated the regression and computed, for each country, each year, and each rating agency, the estimated probability that a country had the highest ranking.[c] I then plotted the estimated probability against the ratio of debt to GDP for each country/year/rating agency. The scatter, shown in figure 4.1, yields a simple and strong conclusion. Relatively low debt has been a necessary but not a sufficient condition to obtain the highest ranking with high probability.

Look first at the outer envelope of the set of points in figure 4.1. A necessary condition to obtaining the highest ranking with a probability close or equal to one has been to have a debt-to-GDP ratio below approximately 70%. As debt increased beyond this level, the probability of obtaining the highest ranking

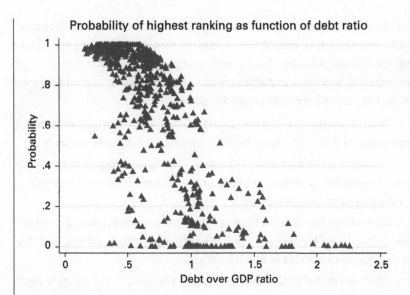

Figure 4.1

Ratings and debt ratios

decreased to approximately 70% for a ratio of debt to GDP of 100%, and 30% for a ratio of debt to GDP equal to 150%. Look, however, at the set of points below this envelope. For many countries, a low debt-to-GDP ratio was not sufficient to ensure a high rating, and other factors dominated.

In short, when examining how rating agencies have assessed debt sustainability in the past, it is clear that they looked at many factors beyond debt. At the same time, they have penalized countries with relatively high levels of debt. The question is whether, in the new low interest rate environment, they will change the relative weights they give to debt versus other factors. (In the rest of the chapter, I am arguing they should.)

---

a. This information is based on Blanchard 2019a, which itself discusses Romer and Romer 2019.

b. See, for example, Afonso, Gomes, and Rother 2011, which is fairly representative.

c. Thanks to Silvia Ardagna for providing the data.

From the point of view of the government, the second step is straightforward. Starting now, what changes can it make to existing or announced policies to reduce the probability of a debt explosion? And if, nevertheless, there is still a need for a sharp adjustment at some point in the future, what measures is the government ready to take?

For outside observers, the second step is more difficult and involves qualitative assessments of whether the measures announced by the government are credible and decrease the risk sufficiently, and if not, whether the government will be willing and able to avoid a debt explosion, were it to appear likely. This in turn depends on many factors:

• It depends on the size of the required adjustment. Having to shift from a large primary deficit to a large primary surplus is likely to be difficult.

• It depends on the maturity of the debt. A longer average maturity gives more time for the government to adjust the primary balance in response to a sustained increase in short rates.

• It depends on the effects of the required fiscal consolidation on output, thus on the room for monetary policy to offset its adverse effects, and thus on the degree to which the ELB is binding.

• It depends on the initial level of taxes. If the level is already very high, the room to increase them is limited.

• It depends on the nature of the government (not just now but also in the future, which makes it hard to predict). A coalition government may be less able to achieve a strong adjustment. So may a parliamentarian system of government.

• It may even depend on the personality of policymakers. For example, the nomination of Mario Draghi as prime minister of Italy in February 2021 clearly reassured markets about debt evolutions in Italy.

In short, assessing debt sustainability is as much art as it is science.

Does this lead one to be nihilistic and to conclude that while simple measures such as debt or current deficits indeed come up short, there is little hope of doing better? I do not think so.

The first step of an SDSA is extremely useful on its own. I have seen this when I was at the IMF. The IMF did not have a full SDSA at the time but instead worked out several alternative scenarios.[14] The discussions about the scenarios were extremely useful. At worst, an SDSA puts together a lot of information and leads to useful discussions about the assumptions—for example, about the distribution of $(r-g)$ or the likelihood that implicit liabilities become explicit.

In the current environment, based on the conclusion reached in chapter 2 that the probability is positive but small that $(r-g)$ will durably reverse

---

14. It is now working on a full SDSA approach. See International Monetary Fund 2021.

sign over the coming decade, the first step is likely to generate for most advanced economies at most a small probability of a rapidly increasing debt, say, 10 years out. But the second step of the process, if needed, is likely to be extremely useful both for governments and for outside observers. It leads governments to think of a plan B in case of an $(r - g)$ reversal.

So far, I have discussed methodology. Turning to content, the logic of SDSAs leads me to draw three major conclusions about the role of debt in affecting debt sustainability in the current environment:

• The main and obvious conclusion is that, just as was the case under the assumption of certainty earlier, $(r - g)$ leads to much more favorable debt dynamics. The presence of uncertainty leads to more prudent conclusions, but moderate primary deficits are unlikely to raise issues of unsustainability.

• If unsustainability is perceived as an issue, the effect of realistic decreases in debt ratios on the probability that debt is sustainable is small. Suppose that a government, through prolonged fiscal austerity, succeeds in reducing the debt ratio over 10 years from 110% to 90% (the goal of returning to 60%, the target debt in the existing European Union (EU) rules, is definitely unreachable over the next decade, short of very high inflation and very low nominal rates). And suppose that $(r - g)$ jumps from −3% to 0%, leading to a corresponding increase in debt service. Absent the adjustment in debt, the increase in debt service is 3.3% of GDP; however, given the debt adjustment, it is still 2.7%—not a large difference in exchange for a long and potentially painful period of fiscal austerity.

• By contrast, the effect of a good contingent plan—for instance, a credible plan to improve the primary balance if $(r - g)$ were to become less favorable by being ready to increase the value-added tax (VAT) rate—has a much larger effect on debt sustainability. If, for example, debt is sustainable under the currently low $(r - g)$, a contingent plan to improve the primary balance one-for-one, but with some distributed lag, in response to a persistent increase in $(r - g)$ eliminates issues of debt sustainability altogether.[15]

---

15. I am conscious of the difficulty of having credible contingent plans. How credible such a plan is depends on the source of the increase in $r - g$. A decrease in underlying potential growth may make it politically difficult to achieve a reduction in the deficit. An increase in r, if it reflects an increase in r^* and an increase in aggregate demand, makes it easier to reduce deficits without adverse effects on output. But the basic conceptual point is clear.

To summarize: A two-step stochastic debt sustainability analysis is the best way to discuss and assess debt sustainability. In the current environment in which low $(r-g)$ is a likely but not certain outcome, a contingent policy to improve the primary balance in response to increases in $(r-g)$ is a better way to ensure debt sustainability than a long period of fiscal austerity in anticipation of a potential increase.

How an SDSA may look—and some implications

It is interesting to show how, in a simple simulation, the results of an SDSA might look like and to strengthen two of the conclusions in the text.[a] To begin, use the following assumptions:

Assume that $(r-g)$ is the sum of a random walk, x, with small variance, and a white noise term, u:

$$(r-g) = x + u$$

$$x = x(-1) + e_x, \ e_x \sim \mathcal{N}(0, s_x), \ x_0 = 0.0$$

$$u = a_u + e_u, \ e_u \sim \mathcal{N}(0, s_u), \ e_u \text{ and } e_x \text{ uncorrelated.}$$

This captures the notion that while expected future $(r-g)$ is equal to its value today, it may either increase or decrease over time either permanently (if e_x) or temporarily (if e_u).

Choose the following calibration:

Assume $s_x = 0.3\%$. The standard deviation of x, n periods ahead, call it $\sigma(x_n)$, is equal to $\sqrt{(n)} * s_x$. Assume that the horizon of the simulation n is 10 years. So, $\sigma(x_n) = 3.3 * s_x = 1\%$, and the probability that the permanent component of $(r-g)$, x_n increases by 2% or more over the 10 years is equal to 2.5%.

Take a_u—the value of $(r-g)$ today (at time 0, before the realizations of e_u and e_x)—to be -2% and the standard deviation of the white noise component s_u to be 1%.

The debt accumulation equation (i.e., ignore the $(1+g)$ term for simplicity) is given by

$$b - b(-1) = (r-g)\,b(-1) - s.$$

Assume the primary balance s to equal a constant a_s plus white noise e_s, plus a feedback term allowing the primary balance to respond to debt service, as discussed in the text:

$$s = a_s + e_s + c\,[(r-g)\,b(-1)], \ e_s \sim \mathcal{N}(0, s_s), \ e_s \text{ uncorrelated with } e_u \text{ and } e_x.$$

Start with a benchmark in which there is no feedback, so c is equal to zero. The exercise is then to compute the probability distribution of debt and the

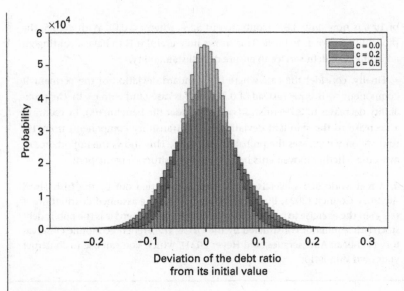

Figure 4.2
Distribution of the change in the debt ratio

deficit n years out. Assume that b_0 is equal to 100%, and that the primary balance is $a_s = -2\%$. Together with the assumption that $a_u = -2\%$, this implies that under certainty ($s_x = s_u = s_s = 0$), the debt ratio would remain constant.

Take the increase in debt by year 10, ($b_{10} - b_1$), as a measure of debt explosion. Figure 4.2 gives its distribution based on 1,000,000 draws for e_x, e_u, e_s. The distribution with the lowest peak and the fattest tails corresponds to the case where $c = 0.0$. The other two correspond to positive values of c and are discussed below.

Under this benchmark, the probability p that the increase in the debt ratio over 10 years exceeds 10% is 5.8%. Now consider alternatives:

- Suppose initial debt is 0.9 rather than 1. Then, the probability of an increase of debt in excess of 10% *increases* to 7.8%! That lower debt would increase the probability of a debt increase is surprising. But it is not a mistake in logic or in programming. When $(r - g)$ is negative, which, starting from −2%, is likely to remain true for a while, investors are in effect willing to pay to hold the debt, and lower debt is bad. One should not make too much of the result, but it indicates that lowering debt may not be that useful.

- Consider instead the case where the primary balance adjusts in part to debt service, defined as $(r - g) b(-1)$, so c is positive. With $c = 0.2$, the distribution is substantially narrower, and thus the probability of a debt increase in excess of 10% is now only 3.8% (compared to 5.8% when $c = 0.0$). With $c = 0.5$, the probability is down to 0.8%. This shows how useful it is to have a contingent adjustment to debt service to ensure debt sustainability.

• Finally, consider the case where the standard deviation of the permanent component, s_x is 0.2% instead of 0.3%. In this case (and with $c = 0$), the probability decreases to 2.7% (instead of 5.8% under the benchmark). By contrast, a decrease in the standard deviation of the transitory component, from 1% to 0.5% only decreases the probability to 4.4%. This shows the importance of assessing whether movements in $(r - g)$ are transitory or permanent.

---

a. A real-world SDSA exercise for Ireland was carried out by the Irish Fiscal Advisory Council (2021, Box H)—although I find the assumed distribution of $(r - g)$ in the exercise to be too wide. Another relevant exercise is the public debt stochastic simulator constructed by the OFCE, the French Economic Observatory (Timbeau Aurissergues, and Heyer 2021), which you can use to construct your own simulation.

4.3   Can One Design Good Sustainability Rules?

What I have suggested doing is an assessment, not a rule. Conceptually, designing a debt sustainability rule is far from obvious.

One needs to distinguish between two types of rules: rules to conduct fiscal policy and rules to ensure debt sustainability. These do not have the same goal. What we are talking about in this chapter, as well as in the discussion of the EU rules, is the second type: leaving countries to follow their preferred fiscal policy while making sure that they do not raise issues of sustainability, which would affect other members.[16] A country may well have a lot of fiscal space—that is, it may be able to support higher debt and deficits—but it may decide not to use the space (think Germany). In that sense, these fiscal rules are different from the monetary policy rules—say, the Taylor rule—or the average inflation targeting (AIT) rule just adopted by the Fed.

This introduces an obvious conceptual issue: Fiscal space, and equivalently debt sustainability, depends on actual current and intended fiscal policy. For example, a credible commitment to decrease primary deficits in

---

16. This distinction is not always made clear in the discussion of EU rules.

the future in response to higher interest rates, were they to increase, will increase the probability that debt is sustainable and give more fiscal space today. This was clear in one of the simulations above: Given the level of debt and primary balance today, making the primary balance contingent on debt service in the future led to a tighter distribution of future debt and a smaller probability that the increase in debt would exceed a given threshold. Two countries with the same debt and deficit today may have very different fiscal spaces.

This is not an issue with the SDSA approach described in section 4.2. Each SDSA is done in situ, for each country and for each year. Thus, it can take into account specific current and announced policies, such as a credible commitment to adjust the primary balance based on debt service evolutions. But it is much more of an issue when designing rules: by their nature, rules cannot come close to capturing all the elements that are captured in an SDSA.

If the goal were to write a rule that simply ensured debt sustainability, this would indeed be easy. One just would need to be extremely conservative. For example, a rule that the deficit must always be equal to zero, along the lines of the German "black zero," would do the job. And, at least on paper, so would rules such as the initial Maastricht rules. But they would do so by unnecessarily constraining fiscal policy. This is why the EU rules have not been respected and, even with all their extensions, are widely considered unacceptable today. The challenge is to find rules that ensure sustainability but leave enough space to use fiscal policy optimally—for example, leave enough room to react to fluctuations in output, especially if there are constraints on monetary policy such as the ELB.

With these considerations in mind, Jeromin Zettelmeyer, Alvaro Leandro, and I have argued that the EU should get rid of formal quantitative rules and follow the approach sketched above. We argued that the EU commission, in combination with national fiscal councils, should do step 1 of the SDSA; that this should be followed by interactions and discussions with the relevant country, followed by step 2, if relevant; and finally, that there should be an adjudication process, either at the Council of the European Union or a new specialized section of the Court of Justice, to require the country to present an adjustment plan or to be penalized in some way (Blanchard, Leandro, and Zettelmeyer 2021). I still believe this is the best way to go. But many policymakers are worried that this may be too weak an approach, that it may lead to unending disagreements and discussions, and they believe that formal quantitative rules are needed.

This has led to many reform proposals.[17]

Some of the proposed reforms are a minima: for example, keeping the 60% debt target but relaxing the constraint on the speed of adjustment to the target, or increasing the debt target to a more realistic level. Many have suggested expenditure rules, aimed at allowing for a stronger fiscal reaction to fluctuations, by constraining spending through the expenditure rule but allowing for revenues to move cyclically, possibly more than implied by the automatic stabilizers.

In principle, one could and should set up the problem as a constrained maximization problem. Which of the large set of variables in the SDSA can be measured? Which ones affect the probability of sustainability the most? What is the cost of leaving out those that cannot be measured? This has not been done. Given where we are, what might be the contours of an acceptable rule?

• The search for simple rules is understandable but quixotic. This is the lesson to be drawn from the history of EU rules. The rules were simple to start, but as time went on and their shortcomings became evident, they became more and more complex. Few people can understand them today (for an attempt at description, see Blanchard, Leandro, and Zettelmeyer 2021). For an analogy, see the picture of the Cathedral of Avila in figure 4.3, which shows the successive additions to the cathedral across the centuries. But their complexity reflects the complexity of reality and the needed assessment, not an excessive complexity of the rule.

• The analysis of debt dynamics above suggests a simple starting principle, however. Go back to equation (4.2). Whether debt is sustainable depends on generating a primary balance s sufficient to cover debt service, defined as $((r-g)/(1+g))b(-1)$. To avoid an increase in the debt ratio, the government must generate a primary balance sufficient to cover debt service so defined.

• This suggests a rule making the primary balance a function of debt service, defined as $((r-g)/(1+g))b(-1)$, with one-to-one pass-through in the

17. See, for example, Bénassy-Quéré et al. 2018 and the references in Blanchard, Leandro, and Zettelmeyer 2021.

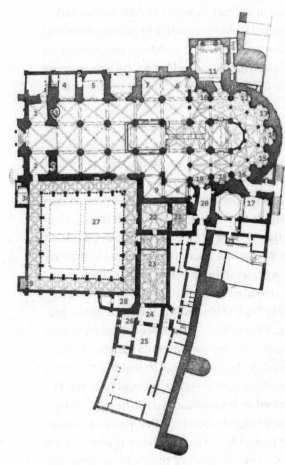

1. Capilla de san Miguel
2. Capilla de san Andrés
3. Pila bautismal
4. Capilla de la Piedad
5. Capilla de la Concepción
6. Capilla de san Antolín
7. Capilla de san Pedro
8. Capilla de santa Teresa
9. Capilla de san Ildefonso
10. Capilla de san Rafael
11. Capilla del Sagrado Corazón
12. Capilla de san Nicolás
13. Capilla de Santiago
14. Capilla de Nª Sª de Gracia
15. Capilla de san Juan Evangelista
16. Capilla de san Esteban
17. Capilla de san Segundo
18. Capilla de la Asunción
19. Capilla de san Juan Bautista. Acceso a las dependencias del Cabildo
20. Sacristía románica
21. Capilla del Sagrario / Antesacristía
22. Capilla de san Bernabé / Sacristía
23. Librería / Capilla Quiroga
24. Atrio del Capítulo nuevo / Sala de los Cantorales
25. Sala capitular nuevo
26. Antiguo archivo catedralicio / Sala de la Pasión
27. Claustro
28. Capilla de las Cuevas
29. Capilla de Nª Sª de la Claustra
30. Capilla del Crucifijo

Figure 4.3
The Cathedral of Avila

long run. Given that movements in the average interest rate on debt can be abrupt (less so the longer the average maturity of the debt), it makes sense to allow the adjustment of the primary balance to happen gradually, rather than at once.[18]

---

18. This is a natural extension of the so-called *Bohn rule* (from the seminal paper by Bohn 1998) showing that a rule that made the primary balance an increasing function of the level of debt would make debt stationary. Bohn also showed that, for

- The shift from casting a fiscal debt limit in terms of debt service rather than debt is a fundamental conceptual change, relative to existing rules that focus on debt. (To reinforce this message, in the summary presentation of the 2021–2022 budget, the US government has added to the line showing the forecast for debt as a ratio to GDP another line showing the forecast for debt service as a ratio to GDP.)[19]

- Should there be a role for debt in addition to debt service? The rule suggested above implies that the process for the debt ratio has a unit root,[20] and one may want to limit movements in the debt ratio through a feedback coefficient of the debt ratio on the primary balance. One reason is that there is, even just for political reasons, an upper limit on how large a primary surplus the government can sustain. If there is such a limit, call it s_{max}, then this, together with the distribution of $(r-g)/(1+g)$, leads to an upper limit on debt. To be concrete, suppose that the maximum sustainable primary surplus is 3% of GDP and that with small but positive probability, $((r-g)/(1+g)$ can reach 2%. Then the maximum sustainable level of debt is given by $b_{max} = s_{max}(1+g)/(r-g) = 3\%/2\% = 150\%$. This is the spirit of the proposal by Martin, Pisani-Ferry, and Ragot 2021: Construct a maximum level for the debt ratio along these lines, building in addition a margin of safety; then, aim not to exceed this level of debt over time. In making the target debt ratio a function of the distribution of $(r-g)$, and possibly of the factors determining s_{max}, this is indeed an improvement over the existing 60% EU debt target. The analysis above suggests, however, that within a realistic range, the effect of debt on the probability of sustainability is small, so the feedback coefficient of debt on the primary balance should be small as well.

- Finally, the rule should have some flexibility, allowing for increases in debt ratios if justified for macro-stabilization purposes. If, for example, private demand is very low, and the policy rate is constrained on the downside by the ELB, it could be that the government must run such

---

the United States, that rule appeared to be satisfied: higher debt led on average to a higher primary balance.

19. Furman and Summers (2020) also focus on debt service, which they define, however, as $rb(-1)$, rather than $((r-g)/(1+g))b(-1)$ as I do here, and they offer a related proposal: As long as debt service remains under 2% of GDP, fiscal policy is free of constraints. If debt service exceeds 2%, then the debt ratio should slowly decrease over time.

20. Suppose, for example, that the primary balance is set equal to debt service, plus unavoidable white noise: $s = ((r-g)/(1+g))b(-1) + \epsilon$. Then $b - b(-1) = -\epsilon$.

large primary deficits to sustain demand that, even with the favorable debt dynamics (as r is low), the debt ratio increases. As argued in chapter 5, the optimal policy may well be in this case to run those primary deficits and let the debt ratio increase for some time; the rule should thus take into account whether or not the ELB constraint is binding.[21]

Similarly, and for the usual reasons, it may make sense to state the rule in terms of the cyclically adjusted primary balance. This raises the issue of measuring whether changes in output are permanent or transitory, which is a difficult issue but one that cannot be avoided.

To summarize: I am skeptical of the use of quantitative rules to ensure debt sustainability. If rules are nevertheless going to be used, then a rule that makes the primary balance adjust over time to debt service is the direction to explore. (I return to the issue of the reform of EU rules after the discussion of public investment in section 4.4.)

4.4 Public Investment and Debt Sustainability

Public investment has often been the victim of fiscal austerity: It is politically easier to cut spending that does not have an effect today than it is to cut transfers for example.

Decisions about public investment should proceed under a separation principle:

• First, whether or not financed by debt, public investment should proceed until the risk-adjusted social rate of return on the investment is equal to the real borrowing rate of the government over the life of the project.[22]

• Second, whether public investment affects debt sustainability depends on the financial returns accruing to the government, either directly or

---

21. This raises the issue of what happens if private demand remains structurally weak, the central bank remains at the ELB, and primary deficits have to be so large as to lead to a steady increase in debt. At some point, debt sustainability can become an issue. I return to the issue after discussing optimal fiscal policy in chapter 5, and again in chapter 6, when I discuss fiscal policy in Japan.

22. This is a simplification; to the extent that the public investment project does not generate market returns for the state and thus will have to be financed in part by a combination of debt and taxes, the decision should also take into account the marginal cost of taxation. To the extent that the investment also has adverse distributional implications, those should also be taken into account.

indirectly. Even if they have high social returns, most public investment projects have either no financial returns or financial returns that are lower than market returns; this is indeed typically the reason why these investments are carried by the public sector. As such, public investments with low financial returns influence debt sustainability.

These considerations yield a clear conclusion. If a public investment yields no financial returns to the government, then, from the point of view of debt sustainability, it will have the same adverse effect on debt sustainability as government consumption. Even if expected financial returns are equal to expected market returns, uncertainty about those returns may still affect the distribution of future debt and thus debt sustainability. Thus, as desirable as public investment is, the proposition that it can be automatically financed by debt is wrong. It may affect debt sustainability and thus may have to be financed in part by taxes.[23]

One practical issue is whether one should take into account indirect financial returns through the effects of public investment on potential output and thus on government revenues in general, even if the investment does not yield direct financial returns to the state. The issue is that such effects are typically hard to assess with any precision ex ante, and the risk is that the government will overstate the positive output effects. For this reason, I believe that assessing these indirect effects should be left to an independent authority. Alternatively, if this is difficult, only in clear-cut cases should these indirect effects be considered. In any case, the uncertainty associated with these effects should be taken into account.[24]

All the effects of public investment on debt dynamics will in principle be captured by an SDSA, and thus there may not be a need for doing more. However, to make public investment more visible and thus less subject to cuts when a government embarks on fiscal austerity, it makes sense to separate the government budget into a current account and a capital account. Also, if a fiscal rule is introduced and puts constraints on the primary balance, the current account primary balance provides a better measure than the overall government primary balance.

---

23. I therefore disagree with the version of the so-called golden rule of public finance that allows capital account spending to be automatically and fully financed by debt.
24. Assessing these indirect effects is known as "dynamic scoring" and has sometimes been taken into account by the CBO in its debt projections since 1997.

One way to think about what a current and a capital account might look like is to think of creating a government agency formally in charge of public capital and separate its account from that of the central government. (This may be a blueprint for setting up a European debt agency.) The separate accounting can take place without an explicit agency in charge, but it makes it simple to describe, and the existence of a formal agency is likely to increase the credibility of the separation between the two accounts. (The algebra and its implications are given in the box, "The algebra of the separation between current and capital accounts.")

So, think of a government agency in charge of public investment and public capital. On the spending side of the agency's income statement is gross investment spending. On the revenue side, the agency has two sources of revenues, apart from debt issuance: gross financial returns from public capital and, as these are typically less than market returns plus depreciation, transfers from the government to provide the difference between the two. The agency issues debt as needed, to finance the difference between revenues and investment. Under this arrangement, the agency debt is fully backed by the revenues from public capital and the transfers from the central government.

Think now of the central government income statement. In the absence of separating current and capital accounts, government spending includes, in addition to interest payments on debt, both government consumption and government investment. Government revenues include, in addition to taxes, financial returns from public capital. In the new central government income statement sheet, spending does not include public investment; revenues do not include financial returns to public capital—both show up on the agency's balance sheet. What appears, however, on the spending side is the transfers from the central government to the agency. To the extent that financial returns are less than market returns plus depreciation, those transfers are positive, reducing the primary balance of the central government and potentially affecting debt sustainability. An SDSA will indicate the room for debt as opposed to tax finance. How and whether this room, if it exists, should be used, and what mix of debt and taxes should be used, will be discussed in chapter 5. A rule, based on the adjustment of the primary balance to debt service, may want to use this definition of the primary balance rather than the standard one.

The algebra of the separation between current and capital accounts

Consider the standard budget constraint of the government. On the expenditure side, separate primary spending into consumption spending and investment spending, and on the revenue side, separate revenues into taxes and financial returns from public capital (assume output growth equal to zero for notational simplicity). Write it as follows:

$$b - b(-1) = (c_g + i_g) - (\tau + x\,k(-1)) + r\,b(-1), \tag{4.3}$$

where c_g is public consumption, i_g is public investment, k is public capital, τ is taxes, and x is the financial rate of return on public capital. Public capital accumulation is given by

$$k - k(-1) = i_g - \delta\,k(-1), \tag{4.4}$$

where δ is the depreciation rate.

The financial rate of return (as opposed to the social rate of return) on public capital is typically less than the market rate of return on private capital, so $x \leq r + \delta$. For many public investments, x is indeed equal to zero.

Now separate the overall account into a current and a capital account. It is easiest to think of a government agency that invests i_g, receives the financial returns from public capital $x\,k(-1)$, and receives transfers from the central government if returns are less than market returns $((r + \delta) - x)\,k(-1)$. The agency can issue debt, b_a. The equation for agency debt dynamics is given by

$$b_a - b_a(-1) = (i_g - x\,k(-1) - ((r + \delta) - x)\,k(-1)) + r\,b_a(-1), \tag{4.5}$$

or, equivalently,

$$b_a - b_a(-1) = i_g - (r + \delta)k(-1) + r\,b_a(-1). \tag{4.6}$$

The central government spends c_g, transfers $(r + \delta - x)\,k(-1)$ to the agency, receives taxes, and issues debt b_c. The equation for the central government debt dynamics is given by

$$b_c - b_c(-1) = c_g + (r + \delta - x)\,k(-1) - \tau + r\,b_c(-1). \tag{4.7}$$

Assume that initially debt is transferred to the agency in relation to its capital, so $b_a(0) = k(0)$, Putting $k(0) = b_a(0)$ in equation (4.6) gives $b_a(1) - b_a(0) = k(1) - k(0)$. Thus, $b_a = k$ from then on. Agency debt is equal to public capital and is fully backed up by the revenues from capital and the transfers from the central government.

One can thus focus on central government debt and primary balance. If the financial rate of return on a public investment is low, transfers to the agency will have to be high and the primary balance will be lower, potentially affecting debt sustainability. In short, public investment will typically affect debt sustainability.

Note that, under this arrangement, there is no incentive for the government to categorize components of c_g as investment (e.g., the salaries of teachers), at least for debt issuance purposes. As they do not yield direct financial returns, shifting them to the agency simply increases the required transfers from the central budget and does not change the debt dynamics of the central government.

The reform of EU rules

The Covid crisis has led to the temporary suspension of EU budget rules, and those rules will probably be reformed before being reinstated. While consultations are still going on and no decision has been taken, there seems to be emerging a political consensus (or at least some political support) for keeping the rules, or at least the 3% deficit and 60% debt numbers enshrined in the Maastricht Treaty, but allowing in parallel for a green investment budget, partly at the national and partly at the EU level, along the lines of the Next-GenerationEU package introduced by the European Union in 2021, financed by debt.

This would be an improvement over existing rules and might balance the desire by some to return to the rules and by others to finance public investment, but it would be far from the best reform.

Given that the official deficit is equal to the primary deficit plus nominal interest payments, one can rewrite the 3% limit on the official deficit, $s - ib(-1) \geq -3\%$ as $s \geq ib(-1) - 3\%$. It is interesting to compare this to the rule we discussed in section 4.3, which can be written (ignoring for simplicity's sake the $(1 + g)$ term) as $s \geq (r - g)b(-1)$ or, using the identity relating the real interest rate, the nominal rate, and the inflation rate $r = i - \pi$, as $s \geq ib(-1) - (g + \pi)b(-1)$. The difference between the two rules is the presence of a fixed 3% in the first versus a term equal to nominal growth $g + \pi$ times debt, $b(-1)$, in the second. Thus, one can think of the 3% rule as a primitive and inferior version of a better rule—but perhaps one easier to explain.

The 60% debt ratio target was always arbitrary. For nearly all EU members, the increase in debt has made it unattainable any time soon. The analysis in this chapter has shown that there is no such thing as a universal threshold over which debt becomes unsustainable, and that the relevant debt level depends on many factors, in particular the real interest rate on debt. Thus, it would be a major mistake to keep both the target and the required speed of adjustment to the target (1/20th of the distance between the actual debt ratio and 60%). Thus, while the 60% ratio may remain as a symbolic and distant target, the weight put on debt reduction should be extremely small.

Finally, while public investment should indeed be a high priority, allowing all such investment to automatically be financed by debt would not be wise. As discussed in this section, even if such investment has high social returns, the absence of financial returns to the state implies that, from the point of view of debt sustainability, there is no difference between, say, the wages of public employees and public investment. Both can potentially threaten debt sustainability, and whether public investment can be financed by debt should not be taken as a given. Furthermore, such a debt pass might lead governments to use too generous a definition of investment, or instead it may lead countries to agree on too limited a list of qualifying projects—for example, excluding measures to fight pandemics, improve medical care, or improve education.

4.5 Multiple Equilibria and the Role of Central Banks

So far (in chapter 3 and in the description of the SDSA in this chapter), I have assumed that interest rates reflected fundamentals—that is, saving/investment and risk/liquidity. What I ignored is that the equilibrium may not be unique and that, in addition to the equilibrium I focused on— call it the "good" equilibrium—there is another "bad" equilibrium, with the same fundamentals but a higher interest rate.

The argument is familiar: Take the case where a government debt is considered safe, the government can thus borrow at the safe rate, and, under these conditions, its debt is considered sustainable. If, however, investors start to worry about default risk—or worry that other investors worry—and then start asking for a risk premium to hold the debt, the higher interest rates and the worsening of the debt dynamics may well increase the probability of default, potentially triggering the very outcome they feared.[25]

As a matter of theory, the bad equilibrium can happen without any change in fundamentals (and thus is often referred to as a sunspot equilibrium). In reality, it is likely to involve both a possibly small perceived deterioration of fundamentals and thus a worsening of the "good" equilibrium leading also to a shift from the good to the bad equilibrium and a large increase in rates.

---

25. A formalization of such debt crises, and their dependence on the level of debt and its maturity, is given by Lorenzoni and Werning 2019.

Such large jumps in rates are not just a theoretical worry. The history of emerging markets is full of examples of "sudden stops" in which investors, in response to some news about fundamentals, try to leave the market en masse, leading to a very large increase in rates and, in some cases, triggering debt default. As has been made clear during the euro crisis, however, such sudden stops can also happen in advanced economies.

This has been used as an argument to decrease debt from its current levels: Lower debt implies a smaller adverse effect of a given interest rate increase on debt dynamics. If debt is sufficiently low, then, even if investors were to worry and require a higher risk premium, this may not be enough to make debt unsustainable and justify the investors' worries. Thus, there may be no bad equilibrium (at least no bad equilibrium under the assumption of rational expectations).

The question becomes: How low is low enough? Based on ongoing work (Blanchard, Kister, and Huertas 2021), the conclusion is: very low. The basic algebra behind the result is given in the box, "Multiple equilibria and safe levels of debt," which derives the upper bound on the value of the debt ratio such that a bad equilibrium cannot exist, both in a one-period and a multiple-period framework. The intuition can, however, be easily given. If investors worry and expect future investors to have similar worries, the sustained increase in interest rates easily leads to an eventual debt explosion. In the example below (which is admittedly too rough to serve even as a benchmark but shows the logic behind the result), if the debt ratio that keeps debt stable under the low interest rate equilibrium (the good equilibrium) is 100%, and if the haircut conditional on default is 30%, the bad equilibrium can arise for debt ratios as low as 7%.

Multiple equilibria and safe levels of debt

Assume that if debt next period, $b(+1)$, exceeds some level, call it b^*, the government defaults, and the haircut on debt is equal to $x, x > 0$.

Let p be the probability of default. Let R denote the stated interest rate on what may now be risky debt. The expected return on debt is therefore given by

$$(1-p)(1+R)+p(1+R)(1-x).$$

Assume that investors are risk neutral and that the safe rate is equal to r. Investors will then require a stated rate R, such that

$$(1+r)=(1-p)(1+R)+p(1+R)(1-x).$$

Solving for R gives

$$(1+R) = \frac{1+r}{1-px}, \text{ implying a spread of } (1+r)\frac{px}{1-px}.$$

Ignoring growth for simplicity's sake, so $g = 0$, debt dynamics are given by:

$$b(+1) = \frac{1+r}{1-px} b - s(+1). \tag{4.8}$$

Ignore uncertainty in s, so $s(+1)$ is equal to some constant s, and thus ignore intrinsic uncertainty in $b(+1)$ (so we focus just on the multiplicity of equilibria).

The equilibrium is characterized by two equations: equation (4.8) above, giving $b(+1)$ as a function of p, and the equation giving p as a function of $b(+1)$ and b^*, as follows:

$$p = 0 \text{ if } b(+1) \leq b^*, \, p = 1 \text{ if } b(+1) > b^*. \tag{4.9}$$

Both equations are represented in figure 4.4, with $b(+1)$ on the vertical axis and p on the horizontal axis.

$b(+1)$ is an increasing convex function of p. The value of $b(+1)$ when $p = 0$ is $(1+r)b - s$. The value of $b(+1)$ when $p = 1$ is $((1+r)/(1-x))b - s$.

p is a step function of $b(+1)$, equal to zero for $b(+1) \leq b^*$, equal to 1 if $b(+1) > b^*$.

Depending on the value of debt today, b, there is either one equilibrium or three (rational expectation) equilibria.

If $b \leq (b^* + s)(1 - x)/(1 + r)$, as in the lower dashed line, the only equilibrium is $p = 0$. Even if investors expect default for sure and ask for a large spread, debt next period is still less than b^*, so $p = 1$ is not a (rational expectation) equilibrium.

If $b > (b^* + s)/(1 + r)$, as in the upper dashed line, the only equilibrium is $p = 1$. Even if investors expect no default, next period debt exceeds b^*, and thus $p = 0$ is not an equilibrium

If b, debt today, is in between those two values, then there are three equilibria: A, B, and C in figure 4.4. B and its associated probability p_B can be excluded on grounds of stability (if investors assume a value of p close to the value of p_B and compute the new probability this implies, they will move away from B toward either A or C). This leaves two equilibria, A and C.

Suppose we take $b^* = 1$ and $r = s = 3\%$, then the highest value of debt today for which there is no default is given by $\hat{b} = (b^* + s)(1 - x)/(1 + r) = 1 - x$. If the haircut, x, is 30%, then the range of values of debt for which there are multiple equilibria goes from 0.7 to 1.

This one-period example is too optimistic, however. Suppose we move to a multi-period model. If investors next period assume that, if following period debt exceeds b^*, there will be default, then there will be default next period when debt exceeds $\hat{b}$. So, coming back to the current period, $\hat{b}$ becomes the

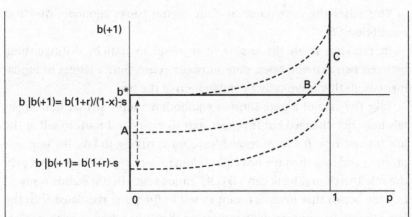

Figure 4.4
The scope for multiple equilibria

new b^*, the critical value above which there is default. As we move back more and more periods, the critical value will decrease until $\hat{b}$ and b^* are equal, and the following condition holds:

$$b^* = (b^* + s)(1 - x)/(1 + r),$$

or solving out:

$$b^* = (1 - x)s/(r + x).$$

Using the above values gives $b^* = 0.7 * 3\%/(33\%) = 0.07$, a very low value, delivering a very large range of multiple equilibria, from 0.07 to 1.00.

A more general derivation, introducing fundamental uncertainty and allowing r to be negative, is given in Blanchard, Kister, and Huertas 2021.

This result has a practical and sad implication: There is no hope to decrease debt ratios to such low levels any time soon. Thus, if it is at all costly in terms of output, this cannot be a motivation for embarking on fiscal austerity because the realistic decrease in debt that can be achieved over, say, the next 10 years, will not eliminate the risk.[26]

---

26. One can play devil's advocate. A commitment by the government to decrease debt may lead investors to be less subject to sunspot worries, thus decreasing the probability of a bad equilibrium. But this is far from a mechanical effect, and it is a dangerous one to count on.

This raises the next question: Can central banks eliminate the "bad equilibrium"?[27]

In thinking about the answer, it is useful to start by distinguishing between two extreme cases: pure sunspots versus pure changes in fundamentals. Reality is typically a combination of the two.

Take the case of a pure sunspot equilibrium. Suppose that fundamentals have not changed but investors start to worry and want to sell at the low interest rate. If a large enough investor is willing to take the opposite position and buy, then the bad equilibrium cannot prevail. This is precisely the role the central bank can play. By announcing that it stands ready to buy the bonds that investors want to sell at the price associated with the low interest rate, and credibly indicating that it has deep enough pockets to buy whatever is needed, it can eliminate the bad equilibrium.[28] Remember the famous statement by Mario Draghi in the summer of 2012, when investors were indeed worried about the debt of a number of euro members and a shift to a bad equilibrium: "Within our mandate, the ECB [European Central Bank] is ready to do whatever it takes to preserve the euro. And believe me, it will be enough."[29,30] Indeed, the announcement may well be enough to prevent the investors from selling in the first place, and thus the central bank may not have to actually intervene. A similar conclusion holds that if investors sell not because they worry but because they temporarily need the funds elsewhere—for example, to close other positions, as happened at the start of the Global Financial Crisis. The central bank can simply replace them and limit the increase in interest rates.

Now take the case of a deterioration of fundamentals, which leads investors to ask for a risk premium and therefore a higher interest rate even

---

27. What follows is even more tentative than the rest of the book. I have not heard counterarguments, but I am not absolutely sure that I am right. To use the usual expression, given the importance of the answer, this is a "fruitful area for further research."

28. Formally, the central bank does not have deep pockets, but rather the ability to finance large purchases through the issuance of bank reserves.

29. Speech by Mario Draghi, president of the European Central Bank, Global Investment Conference, London, July 26, 2012, https://www.ecb.europa.eu/press/key/date/2012/html/sp120726.en.html

30. The "whatever it takes" is important. Announcing a commitment to buy a given amount may not be enough. Investors may still want to test that commitment and sell more than the central bank has announced it is willing to buy.

under the good equilibrium. In this case, it is not obvious that the central bank, were it to want to do so, will be able to decrease the risk premium. As this proposition is likely to be controversial, and because it seems to clash with the empirical evidence, let me first state the argument in its pure form.

In contrast to private investors, the central bank is part of the consolidated government. When it buys government bonds, it pays for them by issuing central bank liabilities. These days, these liabilities typically take the form of central bank reserves at the central bank, which pay interest and are held by banks. Thus, looking at the balance sheet of the consolidated government (central government plus central bank), what happens is a change in the composition of its liabilities, with fewer bonds and more central bank reserves, but no change in its overall liabilities. Thus, if investors worried about default risk, they have no reason to worry less than they did before the intervention.[31]

What happens to interest rates on bonds will depend on how investors perceive the seniority of different types of liabilities in case of default. If, for example, they believe that central bank reserves will be more protected from default than bonds and are in effect safer, then the intervention, which leads to an increase in bank reserves, will make the bonds remaining in the hands of private investors more risky and will *increase* rather than decrease their yields! Or, if instead investors expect central bank reserves to stop paying interest in the future and thus lead to an increase in the non-interest-paying money supply, then investors might expect more inflation in the future and thus ask for higher nominal rates on bonds today. Or, if they hold bonds of a certain maturity for maturity matching or other reasons (the so-called preferred habitat theory of bond holdings) and the central bank intervenes in that particular market, interest rates on those bonds may indeed come down, but interest rates on bonds of different maturities will go up.[32] In short, it is not obvious that, in this case, central bank intervention will decrease rates (or prevent them from increasing).

---

31. The argument does not extend to the purchase of private securities. When a less risk-averse investor is willing to buy those securities, the interest rate on these securities will decrease. The central bank is playing the role of an investor who is less risk averse, in this case. Its intervention will decrease the rate, although the transfer of risk may lead to more risk on the balance sheet of the consolidated government.
32. For evidence on the importance of preferred habitat and the preference of specific investors for specific maturities, see Krishnamurthy and Vissing-Jorgensen 2012.

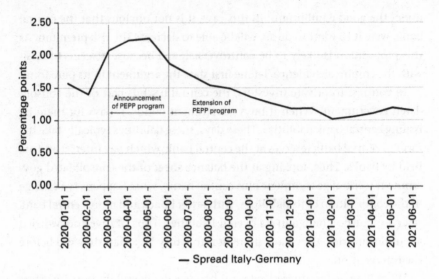

Figure 4.5
The evolution of the spread between Italian and German 10-year bonds since the start of 2020.
Source: Fred.stlouisfed.org.

Yet, going from the theoretical argument to reality, the evidence suggests that central bank interventions have in general decreased spreads. Take ECB interventions during the Covid crisis. Figure 4.5 shows, for example, the evolution of the spread on 10-year Italian bonds relative to German bonds since the beginning of 2020. As the Covid crisis developed, old worries about Italian debt resurfaced, leading to an increase in the spread of Italian over German bonds from February to June of about 80 basis points. In March 2020, the ECB announced a bond purchase program (the Pandemic Emergency Purchase Program, or PEPP) of up to 750 billion euros, extended to 1.3 trillion euros in June, and started buying Italian (and other) government bonds to stabilize and reduce the rates. By early May, despite the intensity of the Covid crisis, the spreads indeed decreased, returning to their pre-Covid level by late summer 2020.

In the light of the theoretical discussion above, why was the ECB successful? Probably for three reasons, the third one being specific to the ECB as opposed to national central banks:

• First, there was probably a large sunspot component to the increase in rates, and investors' worries exceeded what was warranted by fundamentals.

To be fair, the passage of the EU recovery plan in July 2020 improved Italian fundamentals, but the spread had decreased before that.

• Second, investors may have perceived the commitment by the ECB to intervene as a quid pro quo with member governments, in which they committed to take measures to ensure debt sustainability.

• Third, the ECB is more than a national central bank. To the extent that it bought more Italian bonds relative to the capital key—the relative contribution of each euro member to the ECB—which it did, it transferred some of the risk on Italian debt to other euro members.[33]

Overall, I see the discussion serving as a warning about the ability of the central banks to maintain low rates if changes in fundamentals were to put debt sustainability in doubt.

4.6   Central Banks, Bailouts, and Write-Offs

There are two additional issues about the interactions between central banks, fiscal policy, and debt sustainability where I have found the discussion to be often both hot and confused: The first is whether central banks, through quantitative easing, are monetizing the debt and bailing out governments. The second is whether central banks should write off the government bonds they hold to increase fiscal space. The answers to both are a clear no and no.

Debt Monetization and Bailouts

Are central banks, at this juncture, monetizing the debt and bailing out governments, and is this a portend of major inflation to come?

In a sense, central banks have always monetized some of the debt. This is what open market operations aimed at decreasing interest rates have always done. The worry, however, is that central banks are doing this on a completely different scale from the past, in effect financing a substantial part of the large fiscal deficits. For example, since the beginning of 2020, the

---

33. Actually, the scope for such risk transfer is very limited. Under the rules of the PEPP program, the government bonds are bought and held by the national central banks, not by the ECB itself, and in case of default, there is no risk sharing across central banks. Thus, there is redistribution of risk across countries only if investors expect that the rules will not be enforced.

US federal government has run a cumulated deficit of about \$5.9 trillion,[34] and the Federal Reserve (the Fed) has purchased \$3.4 trillion of government securities, an amount equivalent to 57% of the deficit.[35]

The reference to "monetization" in the current context is a misnomer, however. What central banks have typically done is to replace interest-paying bonds with interest-paying central bank reserves, which is quite different from the past when money did not pay interest. The large purchases have no obvious implication for inflation in the future.

Going step by step, let me explain.

First, I want to dispose of an incorrect argument *against* the monetization view. Central banks do not buy newly issued bonds; they buy bonds on the secondary market. Thus, in some formal way, they do not directly finance the government. This is, however, a distinction without a difference. The primary and secondary markets are closely related, and the investors who sell existing bonds to the central bank can use the proceeds to buy the newly issued bonds and keep their portfolios roughly unchanged. It is (nearly) as if the central banks had bought the newly issued bonds directly.[36]

Another argument against the monetization view that I also do not find convincing is lack of intent. During the financial crisis, or during the Covid crisis, central banks have not thought of themselves as directly financing their respective governments. They have thought of themselves as trying to keep interest rates low across all maturities to reflect what the yield curve would have looked like had they been able to achieve the very low neutral rate. Presumably, they would do the same if there were no government deficit but private demand was very weak. This is true, but if in the end, the result has been that they have bought large quantities of government bonds, then intent does not matter per se. It matters, however, for guessing what may happen in the future (more on this below).

---

34. The deficit number is as of the end of 2021. "Federal Surplus or Deficit," FRED Economic Data, St. Louis Federal Reserve Bank, https://fred.stlouisfed.org/series/MTSDS133FMS.

35. Amount as of the end of 2021. "Assets: Securities Held Outright: U.S. Treasury Securities," FRED Economic Data, St. Louis Federal Reserve Bank, https://fred.stlouisfed.org/series/TREAST.

36. The conclusion would be different if the central bank bought the newly issued bonds at below market rates. But this is not the case.

The relevant argument is based on the nature of the liabilities issued by central banks to pay for the purchases of bonds. If these liabilities had been non-interest-paying-money, be it non-interest-paying reserves or currency, then this would have led to a large increase in the non-interest-paying monetary stock, with the potential, if this increase was not undone later, to create high inflation down the road. (This is indeed how hyperinflations have always started). What central banks have issued, however, is interest-paying central bank reserves. To the extent that these pay roughly the same interest rate as the bonds they replace, the effect on overall interest payments of the consolidated government is very small. Governments have not been bailed out by their central banks. As I discussed earlier, central bank intervention does not reduce the overall liabilities of the consolidated government, just their composition. And it does not automatically lead to more inflation: It increases the size of the balance sheet of the central bank, but it does not increase the size of the non-interest-paying money stock. Put another way, we can think of modern central banks as being divided in two activities. The first and traditional one is the issuance of zero-interest money against government bonds or private assets. The second is an intermediary activity, buying public and private assets, and issuing interest-paying central bank reserves. This second activity resembles that of other financial intermediaries and has no direct implication for what happens to inflation.

Given that interest rates are currently very close to zero on both bonds and reserves, the argument that central bank reserves pay interest may seem rather irrelevant at this point: What is the difference between non-interest-paying money and interest-paying money? Indeed, what is important is what will happen if and when the neutral rate increases and the mandate of the central banks is thus to increase the actual rate.

One possibility is that, given the high levels of debt, governments will put pressure on the central bank not to increase rates and debt service even when the neutral rate increases (and the mandate of the central bank would imply that they increase the actual rate in tandem with the neutral rate), an outcome known as *fiscal dominance*. This is indeed a potential worry, but the pressure will depend on the level of debt of the consolidated government (which is what determines interest payments to outside investors and which, as we have seen, is unaffected by central bank purchases), rather than on the size of the balance sheet of the central bank.

Another possibility is that the central bank itself will be reluctant to increase rates. While an increase in rates will increase both outlays (interest paid to banks on central bank reserves) and revenues (interest received on government bonds), the increase in rates implies capital losses on long maturity bonds and might lead to a negative balance sheet for the central bank. From an economic viewpoint, a negative balance sheet is not an issue for the central bank.[37] This is even more the case here, as the capital losses of the central bank on its holdings of government bonds are reflected one-for-one in corresponding capital gains for the government on those very same bonds, leaving the consolidated balance sheet unaffected. But it may be a political issue and lead to a decrease in the central bank's independence. This is certainly something central banks worry about.[38]

To summarize: Central banks are not bailing out governments. The risk is there that high debt leads to fiscal dominance or that large balance sheets with long maturity bonds lead central banks to keep rates too low. But I believe the risk is small. Advanced economies' central banks have shown their independence. The evidence from the increase in rates by the Fed and the Bank of England during the period from 2016 to 2018 is reassuring. In the case of the ECB, the fact that there is not one fiscal authority but rather 19 countries, with different attitudes vis-à-vis fiscal policy and debt, makes fiscal dominance of the central bank extremely unlikely.

Should Central Banks Write Off Their Holdings of Government Bonds?

As debt levels have increased, some have argued that central banks should simply write off their holdings of government bonds to give governments more fiscal space.[39] I have argued earlier that there was a lot of remaining fiscal space, so there was no need for any kind of write-off at this point; but leaving this argument aside, this particular type of write-off would not achieve what its proponents believe.

---

37. A bank that just did helicopter money would have liabilities and no assets, and this would not be an issue.

38. The Fed has avoided this issue altogether by holding bonds to maturity and not marking them to market.

39. This proposition has been particularly salient in France. For example, see the February 2021 statement by 100 economists (in French) at https://economix.fr/uploads/source/media/LeMondeAnnulationtribune.pdf.

The proposition is that the cancellation of the bonds held by the central bank would decrease the amount of interest payments and thus the debt service of governments. And indeed, it would. But it would have another effect—namely, to decrease the revenues of the central bank and thus the profits that the central bank turns in to the government. This second effect would be exactly of the same size as the first, and the net effect on the government budget constraint would be equal to zero.

Another way of stating the same conclusion is to look at the operation from the viewpoint of private investors. From their viewpoint, this is just an exchange of claims between the government and the central bank. The central bank gives up claims on the government; the government gives up claims on central bank profits. This has no implication for private investors. (Some proponents have argued that the decrease in the reported official debt of the central government—which indeed would happen—would lead investors and rating agencies to see this as an improvement and thus increase fiscal space. This is assuming too much stupidity on the part of investors.)

While the write-off has no direct effects, it is likely to have adverse political effects. As a signal, it may lead investors to question the central bank's independence. And given the size of most central bank balance sheets, the cancellation of claims on the government is likely to lead to a negative balance sheet for the central bank. As I discussed earlier, while this is of no economic relevance, it may make it more difficult for the central bank to keep its independence vis-à-vis the government, leading to a higher probability of fiscal dominance. It is to be avoided.

A final remark about the ECB (as this is the context in which the French discussion has taken place). Because the ECB is not a national bank, cancellation of government bonds of one member country would indeed improve the fiscal situation of that country. The reason is that, given that ECB profits are distributed among all member countries (in proportion to their capital key), the decrease in profits for the country whose debt is written off will be much smaller than the decrease in its debt. In effect, the cancellation will lead to a transfer from all member countries to the country in question. This shows, however, the limits of the argument: It is very unlikely that other members will agree to it. And if the debt is canceled in the same proportion for all members, then the same irrelevance result obtains: the decrease in claims held by the ECB on governments will be offset by a decrease in ECB profits going back to the member countries.

4.7 Conclusions

I argued in chapter 3 that $(r - g)$ was likely, although not certain, to remain mostly negative for a long time. The theme of this chapter is that it makes the dynamics of debt much more benign. This does not make the issue of debt sustainability disappear, however, both because of endogeneity and the effect of fiscal policy back on the neutral interest rate and because of uncertainty, in particular with respect to r.

I have argued in this chapter that the best way to assess debt sustainability is through the use of a stochastic debt sustainability analysis, or SDSA, which is an approach that takes into account the specificities of each country and each year. I have argued that, given the complexity of the assessment, I am skeptical that one can rely on quantitative rules. If, however, such rules are used, I suggest that they should be based on requiring the primary surplus to adjust to debt service, defined as $((r - g)/(1 + g))b(-1)$, rather to debt itself. It cannot avoid including exceptions, though, such as the need to allow for larger primary deficits when the central bank is constrained by the ELB.

I have discussed sudden stops and the ability of central banks to limit spreads on government bonds. I have argued that whether or not they can depends very much on the nature of the spreads and whether they reflect fundamental or nonfundamental factors. I have argued that the probability of a bad equilibrium is only marginally influenced by the level of debt, but can be much reduced by a contingent rule making the primary balance react to an increase in debt service.

5 Welfare Costs and Benefits of Debt and Deficits

This chapter begins with what may feel like an abstract and slightly esoteric topic, but, it turns out, the topic is central to the discussion of fiscal policy—namely, the effects of debt on welfare under certainty and then under uncertainty.

Section 5.1 looks at the welfare costs of debt under certainty. Public debt is widely thought of as bad, as "mortgaging the future." The notion that higher public debt might actually be good and increase welfare (on its own, by ignoring what it is used to finance) feels counterintuitive. The section reviews what we know about the answer under the assumption of certainty. The answer is that debt might indeed be good, and that the condition, under certainty, is precisely $(r - g) < 0$. The section puts together the two celebrated steps of the answer. The "golden rule" result, put forth by Phelps 1961, says that if $(r - g) < 0$, less capital accumulation increases welfare; and the demonstration by Diamond 1965, in an overlapping generation model, says that if $(r - g) < 0$, issuing debt does, by decreasing capital accumulation, increase the welfare of both current and future generations. These are clearly important and intriguing results. They are, however, just a starting point.

A major issue is again uncertainty, the issue taken up in section 5.2. Under the assumption of certainty, there is only one interest rate, so the comparison between r and g is straightforward. But, in reality, there are many rates, reflecting their different risk characteristics. The safe rate is indeed less than the growth rate today. But the average marginal product of capital, as best as we can measure it, is substantially higher than the growth rate. Which rate matters? This is very much research in progress, but thanks to a number of recent papers, we have a better understanding of the issue. In the Diamond model, for example, which focuses on finite lives as the potential source of high saving and excess capital accumulation, the relevant rate is typically a combination of the two, although with a major role for the safe rate. Going to the data suggests that the relevant rate and the growth rate are very close, making it difficult to decide empirically on which side of the golden rule we actually are. In other models, where, for example, the lack of insurance leads people to have high precautionary saving, potentially leading to excess capital accumulation, the answer is again that the safe rate plays a major role; in that case, however, while debt is likely to help, the provision of social insurance, by getting at the source of the low r, may dominate debt as a way of eliminating capital overaccumulation. Overall, given what we know, a prudent conclusion is that, in the current context, public debt may not be good but is unlikely to be very bad—that is, to have large welfare costs—and that the more negative $(r - g)$, the lower the welfare costs.

Section 5.3 turns to the welfare benefits of debt and deficits. It focuses on the role of fiscal policy in macro-stabilization, a central issue if, for example, monetary policy is constrained by the effective lower bound (ELB). It reviews what we know about the role of debt, spending, and taxes (and, by implication, deficits) in affecting aggregate demand: Higher debt affects wealth and thus consumption demand. Higher government spending affects aggregate demand directly; lower taxes do so by affecting consumption and investment. Multipliers (i.e., the effect of spending and taxes on output) have been the subject of strong controversies and a lot of recent empirical research. The section discusses what we have learned. The basic conclusion is that multipliers have the expected sign, and fiscal policy can indeed be used to affect aggregate demand.

Section 5.4 puts the conclusions about welfare costs and benefits of debt and deficits together and draws their implications for fiscal policy. One can think of two extreme approaches to fiscal policy. The first, call it *pure public finance*, focuses on the role of debt and deficits, ignoring the effects of fiscal policy on demand and output—for example, by implicitly assuming that monetary policy can maintain output at potential in response to a change in fiscal policy. If, for example, this approach leads to the conclusion that debt is too high, then fiscal policy should focus on debt reduction. The second approach, call it *pure functional finance* (in reference to the name given to it by Abba Lerner 1943), focuses instead on the potential role of fiscal policy in maintaining output at potential, as might be the case if monetary policy is constrained by the ELB. I argue that the right fiscal policy is a mix of these two approaches, with the weight on each one depending on the level of the neutral rate. The lower the neutral rate, the lower the fiscal and welfare costs of debt, on the one hand; the smaller the room of maneuver of the central bank, on the other; and thus the more the focus should be on the pure functional finance approach and on the use of deficits to sustain demand, even if these lead to an increase in debt. The higher the neutral rate, the higher the fiscal and welfare costs of debt, on the one hand; the larger the room of maneuver of the central bank, on the other; and thus the more the focus should be on the pure public finance approach and, if indeed debt is perceived as too high, on a decrease in debt. The section ends by discussing a number of related issues, such as the role of the inflation target and the alternatives to deficits to increase demand if secular stagnation becomes worse.

5.1 Debt and Welfare under Certainty

In 1961, Edmund Phelps argued the following: A market economy could accumulate too much capital. Such overaccumulation would be reflected in a simple inequality, namely $(r - g) < 0$, where r was the net marginal product of capital (and because Phelps was working in the context of a model with no uncertainty, r was also the safe rate of interest). If this condition held, decreasing capital would actually be welfare improving.[1]

To understand his argument, go back to the basic national income identity. (In general, we would have to include government spending, and in an open economy, exports minus imports, but the argument is simpler

---

1. This section and the next rely on growth theory, first under certainty and then under uncertainty. Growth theory can be quite elaborate, and this is not the place to exposit it. I have tried to give the intuition for the basic results with minimal math and rely on footnotes and a couple of boxes to dig a bit deeper. For those familiar with growth theory: The presentation would be more rigorous if I worked with all variables divided by effective units of labor, so all the variables were constant in steady state. I found it hard to explain without getting into a discussion of the specification of the production function and the form of technological progress.

to present if we ignore them for the time being.) Output is equal to consumption plus investment. Or equivalently, consumption is equal to output minus investment:

$$C = Y - I. \tag{5.1}$$

Assume output is equal to potential output, itself given by the production function $F(K,.)$ where the dot denotes other factors of production from labor to an index of the state of technology.

Assume that the economy is on a balanced growth path, so that C, Y, I are all growing at some rate g. Assume that capital depreciates at rate δ, so that for capital to grow at rate g, investment must cover both depreciation and the growth of the capital stock:

$$I = (\delta + g)K.$$

Replacing the terms in equation (5.1) gives

$$C = F(K,.) - (\delta + g)K. \tag{5.2}$$

The effect of additional capital on consumption is thus given by

$$dC/dK = F_K(K,.) - (\delta + g) = (F_K(K,.) - \delta) - g.$$

Taking the interest rate to be equal to the net marginal product of capital, $r \equiv F_K(K,.) - \delta$, the equation above becomes

$$dC/dK = r - g.$$

The relation between capital and consumption at any point along the growth path is represented in figure 5.1. Consumption is an increasing function of capital until $(r - g) = 0$. That level of capital is called the golden rule level of capital. As we look at levels of capital higher than the golden rule level, $(r - g)$ becomes negative and consumption becomes a decreasing function of capital. The intuition is that, as the capital stock increases, depreciation (which needs to be replaced) increases linearly with capital, but the gross marginal product of capital increases at a slower pace so that the net marginal product of capital becomes negative. Although output is higher, so much has to be put aside for investment that what is left for consumption is lower.

Suppose the economy is to the right of the golden rule, so $(r - g) < 0$, and we decrease capital today, leading to more output being left for

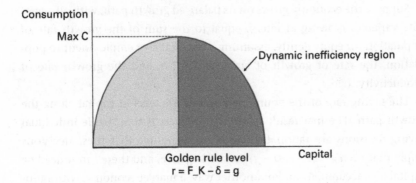

Figure 5.1
Consumption as a function of capital, golden rule, and dynamic inefficiency

consumption.[2] As long as the inequality holds,[3] this will lead to both more consumption today and more consumption in the future. To use the terminology used by Phelps, the economy is *dynamically inefficient*: both current and future generations can be made better off.

Can there really be capital overaccumulation? And why should public debt help in this case?

Diamond (1965), using the same two-period overlapping model as the one we used in chapter 4 to discuss saving and demographics, gave the answers: Even if people are fully rational and take individually optimal saving decisions, there can indeed be capital overaccumulation. If this is the case, then anything that decreases saving can, if distribution effects do not stand in the way, increase everybody's consumption and welfare, now and in the future. Intergenerational transfers, or public debt, can play that role. The argument goes as follows.

Suppose people live for two periods, working in the first, retiring in the second. They receive a wage in the first period, save by investing in capital (so there is no separate saving/investment decision), and consume the capital and the returns from capital in the second period. Thus, the saving of the young determines the capital stock of the economy in the next period.

---

2. We can do so by not replacing part of the depreciated capital.
3. As we decrease capital, the marginal product of capital increases and so does the interest rate. For a large enough decrease in capital, r becomes larger than g, and the inequality changes sign.

Suppose the economy grows on its balanced growth path, with all aggregate variables growing at rate g, equal to the sum of the growth rate of population (or equivalently, assuming a fixed ratio of employment to population, the rate of growth of employment), n, and the growth rate of productivity, x.[4,5]

The saving rate of the young determines the level of capital along the growth path. The first result the model delivers is that, while individual saving decisions are rational, there is no guarantee that these decisions imply that $r = (F_K - \delta) > g$: $(r - g)$ can be negative, and there can indeed be capital overaccumulation. Put another way, a market economy, with rational individuals, can be on the wrong side of the golden rule and thus be dynamically inefficient.

The second result is that, if this is the case, transfers from the young to the old can increase welfare for all generations, current and future:

- When the young save one unit, they get $(1 + r)$ units when old. Now suppose that the government puts in place a transfer scheme, taking D from each of the young and giving $(1 + n) D$ to each of the old within the same period (as there are $(1 + n)$ young for each old), with D increasing at rate x over time. Think of it as a pay-as-you-go retirement system, in which the contributions from the young finance the benefits for the old, and per capita retirement contributions and benefits increase with productivity over time.

- When young, people lose D in income. When old, they receive $D(+1)$ $(1 + n) = D(1 + x)(1 + n) = D(1 + g)$ in income. (Here, $D(+1)$ is the individual transfer from each of the young next period, and there are $(1 + n)$ young workers for every old worker.) If $(r - g) > 0$, the transfer scheme delivers less than saving and thus decreases their welfare. But if $(r - g) < 0$, however, the transfer scheme is more attractive than saving and increases the welfare of each generation. In this case, a pay-as-you-go retirement system can make all generations better off.

Likewise, debt also generates intergenerational transfers, in a slightly different way. Think of the government issuing one-period debt every period,

---

4. More accurately, g is defined by $(1 + g) = (1 + x)(1 + n)$. But, for x and n small, the product xn is very small, and taking g simply as the sum of the two is a good approximation.

5. The original Diamond model did not have productivity growth, but the extension is straightforward and useful for our purposes.

with debt issuance increasing at rate g. The young who buy the debt receive $D(1+r)$ when old and are indifferent between investing in capital or buying the debt, because both pay r. The issuance of debt next period is equal to $D(+1)=D(1+g)$. Thus, each period, the government gets the difference between revenues from debt issuance $D(1+g)$ and payments on debt $D(1+r)$. If $r<g$, this difference, equal to $D(g-r)$, is positive and can be redistributed to a combination of the young and the old, making them better off.

There is a limit to these two schemes, be it pay-as-you-go or debt. As debt decreases capital accumulation, and it has general equilibrium effects. The wage decreases, and the marginal product of capital and thus the interest rate increases. When the interest rate becomes equal to the growth rate, the economy is at the golden rule. Further debt leads to $(r-g)>0$, and debt no longer improves the welfare of all generations. The initial old gain, but the others lose. The government then has to think about the trade-off between the current old, who benefit from debt, and future generations, who face lower consumption and lose from debt. But until this threshold is reached, public debt can improve welfare for all.

These are important, intriguing, and probably to many readers, counterintuitive results that were seen as surprising but exotic outcomes until recently. Could it really be that advanced economies accumulate too much capital? Could public debt really be good for welfare, independent of what is done with it? But the fact that r is now so much lower than g forces us to take these questions more seriously. To give a full answer, one must look at how this analysis extends under uncertainty.

5.2 Debt and Welfare under Uncertainty

In contrast to the maintained assumption of section 5.1, we live in a world of uncertainty, where there are many interest rates and rates of return, from rates on government bonds to the rates of return on equity and so on.

In the discussion of debt sustainability in chapter 4, the rate that was relevant to the discussion was the rate at which the government could borrow, thus in effect the safe rate or close to it in most advanced economies. The welfare discussion in section 5.1 suggests, however, that what is important is instead the marginal product of capital, net of depreciation. And, on average, this rate appears substantially higher than the average growth rate.

Figure 5.2 shows the evolution of two measures of rates of return on capital for the United States since 1992. Both use the same measure of earnings in the numerator—namely, the pretax earnings of US nonfinancial corporations.[6] The dashed line shows the ratio of earnings to the capital stock measured at replacement cost. The black line shows the ratio of earnings to the capital stock measured at market value. Which of the two is a better proxy for the marginal product of capital is not obvious: If there were no rents, then the ratio of earnings to replacement cost would be the natural measure. But some corporate earnings represent rents, and the value of these rents may be why the market value of capital exceeds its replacement cost, in which case using the ratio of earnings to capital at market value seems more appropriate.[7,8,9]

For our purposes, we do not need to choose between the two measures: The point is that either measure of the marginal product is substantially higher than the real safe rate (see figure 3.1) and, more importantly, substantially higher than the growth rate.

This raises the obvious question: Which rate should we choose in assessing the welfare effects of debt?

To answer, think again of the Diamond economy with an underlying constant rate of growth g, but with fluctuations in the marginal product of capital F_K, leading to fluctuations around the growth path in both the

---

6. We care about the returns to capital, not the returns after taxes.

7. Gutierrez and Philippon (2017) discuss the importance (and the increase over time) in rents in the United States. Note also that the ratio of market value to replacement cost is what is known as "Tobin's q," so the figure implies an average value of q of 1.25 over the period. The fact that q is consistently greater than 1 during the period suggests the presence of rents equal to about 25% of the average product of capital.

8. For a discussion of the relation between the marginal product of capital and the profit rate when firms have monopoly power, see Ball and Mankiw 2021. They show that there are two effects at work. Monopoly power in the goods market implies that all factors of production, capital as well as labor, are paid less than their marginal product. Thus payments to capital understate the marginal product of capital. But monopoly power also generates rents, which increase the profit rate. The two effects work in opposite directions, and thus it is not clear whether the profit rate overstates or understates the marginal product of capital.

9. Farhi and Gourio (2019) construct and calibrate a model to account for the decline in the real safe rate, the stability of the rate of return on capital, and several other stylized facts. They conclude that increasing rents, and an increased risk premium, constitute an important part of the overall explanation.

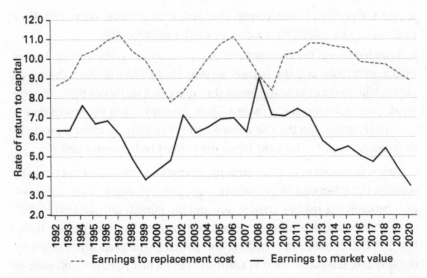

Figure 5.2
Rates of return to capital.
Source: Blanchard 2019b, fig. 15, with data extended to 2020.

marginal product of capital and in output.[10] (The box below, on the effects of a transfer on welfare, gives the basic algebra.) Return to our transfer scheme:

- When the young save one unit, they get $(1 + F_K - \delta)$ units next period.

- Now suppose the government puts in place a transfer scheme, taking D from each the young and giving $(1 + n)D$ to each of the old, with D growing

---

10. By relying on an overlapping generation model without financial frictions, I focus on the "crowding out" effect of debt on capital accumulation and, by implication, on future output. I do so because I believe it is the main effect at work. A parallel line of research has emphasized the potential usefulness of public debt in the presence of financial frictions. If, for example, consumers face borrowing constraints, increasing their current income while decreasing their income later (i.e., financing public spending by debt rather than taxes) can relax these borrowing constraints and increase the consumers' welfare (Woodford 1990). If, for example, firms that want to invest need to post good collateral in order to borrow, public debt can play that role and allow them to borrow more. For papers that explore those effects, see Holmström and Tirole 1998, or Farhi and Tirole 2012. Or, to take a further example, a larger public debt may also increase market liquidity (i.e., the depth and liquidity of the bond market). I do not explore these implications here.

at rate x over time. When young, they lose D in income. When old, they receive $D(+1)(1+n) = D(1+x)(1+n) = D(1+g)$ in income.

- As we have seen, the average value of $(F_K - \delta)$ appears substantially higher than g, so it looks as if the transfer scheme (and by implication, the use of public debt) decreases the welfare of the young. But this is not right. $(F_K - \delta)$ is risky, while the transfer is riskless. Thus, we must adjust the rate of return on capital for risk. But the risk-adjusted rate of return on capital is precisely the riskless rate, r.[11] Thus, the comparison must be between r and g.

This would seem to lead to a striking conclusion: Even under uncertainty, whether the effect of debt on welfare is positive still depends on a comparison between the riskless interest rate and the growth rate; and given that $(r - g) < 0$, public debt has no welfare costs and indeed has welfare benefits.[12,13] This conclusion is striking and points to the deep issues raised by the very low safe rates, but it is again still only a first pass, for a number of reasons:[14]

The effects of a transfer on welfare

Assume that people have the following utility function:[a]

$$\max (1 - \beta)U(C_1) + \beta E[U(C_2)],$$

where C_1 is consumption when young, and C_2 is consumption when old, and $E[U(.)]$ represents expected utility. Their budget constraints are given by:

$$C_1 = W - D - K$$

---

11. Even if people do not actually have access to safe debt, as is the case here, we can ask what rate they would require to hold the safe asset. At the margin, they would have to be indifferent between holding risky capital and the safe asset.

12. See Summers 1990 for an early argument along these lines

13. A nerdy footnote: A counterexample to this conclusion is given by Barro (2021), who shows that in an economy with infinitely long lived but sufficiently risk-averse individuals, the safe rate can be less than the growth rate, while the economy is dynamically efficient. But in that economy, safe debt is in zero supply, and the government, which has no particular advantage over individuals, cannot issue safe debt forever.

14. Warning: The next set of points gets a bit technical. It is also more tentative than other parts of the book. The reader can skip them and go to the bottom line: It is hard to pin down what the right rate should be compared to the growth rate. A prudent conclusion is that, from a welfare viewpoint, debt may be bad but not very bad.

$C_2 = (1 + F_K - \delta)K + (1 + n)(1 + x)D.$

When young, they receive a wage, pay the transfer D to the government, and save by investing K in capital. When old, they consume the proceeds from their investment and the transfer $D(1 + n)(1 + x) = D(1 + g)$ from the government. In the first period they choose how much to save, K. The first order condition with respect to K is given by

$-(1 - \beta)U'(C_1) + \beta E[(1 + F_K - \delta)U'(C_2)] = 0.$

The effects of a transfer on utility are given by

$X = -(1 - \beta)U'(C_1) + \beta(1 + g)E[U'(C_2)].$

They receive higher transfers in period 2 than they pay in period 1, both because there are more young than old and because productivity is higher and transfers increase with productivity. Thus, the presence of $(1 + g)$ in the second term.

Using the first-order condition, X can be written as

$X = \beta((1 + g)E[U'(C_2)] - E[(1 + F_K - \delta)U'(C_2)]).$

The riskless rate (which, in this case, is the shadow rate people would require in order to hold safe debt) satisfies the condition

$(1 + r)EU'(C_2) = E[(1 + F_K - \delta)U'(C_2)].$

Replacing the terms in the equation above gives

$X = \beta(g - r)E[U'(C2)]$, so if $r < g$ then $X > 0.$

If $r < g$, the direct effect of a transfer (or higher debt) is to increase welfare. While the algebra is slightly different, a similar argument applies if the government issues debt rather than runs a transfer scheme.

$a.$ This is a simplified version of the analysis in Blanchard 2019b.

- The argument leaves aside the indirect effects of public debt. As debt is issued and displaces capital in the portfolio of the young, lower capital decreases returns to labor and increases returns to capital, and these in turn affect welfare. The implication of these indirect effects turns out to be complicated, but the conclusion is that, in general, both the safe rate and the average rate of return on capital will matter.[15]

---

15. Nerdy footnote: Similar indirect effects are present in the original Diamond model under certainty, but they reinforce the direct effects. This is not the case here.

In Blanchard 2019b, I derived an approximate formula under the assumption of a Cobb-Douglas production function, which (adapted to allow for underlying growth, which I had left aside in the original article) gives the condition that public debt increases welfare if $1/2\,(r + E(F_K - \delta)) <$ g (where $E(.)$ is now an unconditional expectation), thus giving equal weights to the safe rate and the average marginal product of capital.[16]

Taking this approximation at face value and using a real safe rate of -0.5% (roughly the current 10-year real rate on indexed bonds) and an average real rate of return on capital of 5.5% (roughly the average rate of return on stocks since 1992, measured by the ratio of earnings to market value) gives $1/2\,(r + E(F_K - \delta)) = 2.5\%$, which is close to the expected real growth rate, over the next 10 years, of 2%. This rough computation thus suggests that the effect of debt on welfare through the displacement of capital is probably close to zero.[17]

• The argument assumes that the difference between the safe rate and the expected rate of return on capital reflects investors' rational decisions, based on their degree of risk aversion and the degree of aggregate risk associated with capital. There is, however, substantial controversy about whether this is the case. The issue is known as the *equity premium puzzle*.[18] The puzzle is that, given the observed limited variations in aggregate earnings, it would take an implausibly high degree of risk aversion to explain the size of the equity premium. A version of the puzzle can be seen in figure 5.2: Since

---

16. The relative weights of the safe rate and the average risky rate depend on the elasticity of substitution between labor and capital in production. If technology is linear in labor and capital, the wages and the marginal product are independent of the level of capital, the indirect effects are equal to zero, and the correct rate is the safe rate. The lower the elasticity, the larger the relative weight on the average marginal product of capital. The Cobb-Douglas assumption, which implies a unit elasticity of substitution, is often seen as an empirically reasonable assumption.

17. Martin Hellwig (2021) has shown that a combination of public debt and tax policies to undo the indirect effects on wages and rates of return on capital will increase welfare if $r < g$—namely, the condition derived above considering only the direct effects and involving only the safe rate. This is an important theoretical result but one of limited empirical relevance in thinking about the welfare effects of debt, given that these tax policies are not actually implemented.

18. The standard reference is Mehra and Prescott 1985. The equity premium refers to the difference between the safe rate and the rate of return on stocks, but is directly related to the difference between the safe rate and the expected rate of return on capital as a whole.

1992, the ratio of earnings to capital (at replacement cost or market value) has never been lower than the safe rate. Investors with claims to next period marginal product would have had higher returns in each year than if they held the safe asset. Various explanations have been advanced. Robert Barro has argued that rare, and thus rarely observed, macroeconomic disasters may explain the premium (Barro and Ursua 2011). If so, there may be no puzzle, just a fat tail distribution of shocks. Others have suggested behavioral explanations such as myopic risk aversion (Benartzi and Thaler 1995); if so, one would have to see whether the argument carries through with those preferences and behavior (I have not done this analysis).

• Given the difficulties in assessing what is behind the equity premium, Abel et al. (1989) derived a very intuitive sufficient condition for dynamic inefficiency that does not depend on it: If, every year, gross profits exceeded gross investment, implying a positive net cash flow, then one could be confident that there was no capital overaccumulation. They applied their criterion to six major advanced economies and concluded that this condition was satisfied for every country in every year of the time period they looked at (1953 for the United States, 1960 for the others). The approach has, however, been revisited by Geerolf (2018), who argues that, excluding land rents and entrepreneurial income from gross profits, no advanced economy actually satisfies the sufficient condition, and thus the issue of capital overaccumulation remains open.[19]

• The overlapping generation model used to discuss the issue does not include financial frictions. These frictions exist, however, and individuals face much more risk than aggregate risk. They face substantial idiosyncratic shocks that they cannot fully insure against. In this case, precautionary behavior will lead to more saving, to a lower neutral safe rate, and possibly to a larger equity premium. This does not destroy the case for higher public debt to potentially increase welfare, but, in this case, public debt may not be the best tool. Providing better social insurance, and thus directly addressing the problem of missing insurance markets, is clearly a better way to do it. From a macro viewpoint (i.e., leaving aside the fact that more social

---

19. Another paper reaching similar conclusions is Luo, Kinusaga, and Kajitani 2020. It also reaches a more dramatic conclusion—namely, that China has a profit rate that is smaller than its investment rate and therefore may suffer from capital overaccumulation.

insurance is likely to be welfare improving on its own), "Medicare for all," for example, even if it is fully self-financing, may dominate higher debt. This point will be relevant when we discuss actual policy choices later.[20]

In short, $(r - g) < 0$ is a strong signal that the risk-adjusted return on capital is surprisingly low, and thus the welfare costs of public debt coming from the reduction in the capital stock are also low. The next section turns to potential welfare benefits

5.3 Fiscal Policy, the ELB, and Output Stabilization

Even if monetary policy is unconstrained, fiscal policy can help reduce fluctuations. There is indeed a long tradition of letting automatic stabilizers operate in order to allow for lower tax revenues and higher transfers to stimulate demand when output is unusually low: The argument is that they act faster than monetary policy in affecting demand and output.[21] The case for using fiscal policy is, however, stronger when the nominal policy rate is at the effective lower bound or even when it is positive but low enough that monetary policy cannot offset large adverse shocks.

---

20. Financial frictions and missing insurance markets against idiosyncratic shocks (à la Aiyagari 1994) are indeed an attractive alternative and complementary formalization to overlapping generation models to think about the role of public debt. Kocherlakota (2021) shows that, in such a model, the safe rate r can be less than g, and if this is the case, public debt does improve welfare. See also Aguiar, Amador, and Arellano 2021 for a closely related treatment. Another example along the same lines is given by Brumm et al. (2021), who construct an elegant two-period model with idiosyncratic shocks where indeed the first-best policy is for the government to provide better insurance rather than issue public debt; but even in their model, (some increase in) public debt improves welfare.

21. In practice, automatic stabilizers have been an inadvertent outcome of the structure of taxation and transfers: A higher average tax rate or a more progressive tax and transfer system, for example, leads to stronger stabilizers. For example, a paper from the Organisation for Economic Co-operation and Development (OECD), by Maravalle and Rawdanowicz 2020, finds that the effect of a 1% decrease in output leads to an increase in the budget deficit (or a decrease in the budget surplus, if the country starts with a surplus) of 0.65% of gross domestic product (GDP) for Belgium but only 0.38% for Korea. In other words, the automatic stabilizers are nearly twice as strong in Belgium as in Korea. There is general agreement that these automatic stabilizers can and should be improved (Blanchard and Summers 2020; Boushey, Nunn, and Shambaugh 2019).

The question, then, is whether and how fiscal policy affects aggregate demand and in turn output.[22]

One must distinguish between three channels: the effect of debt itself, the effect of taxes and transfers, and the effect of government spending. For those who hold the debt, public debt is part of their wealth and thus affects their consumption. Current and future taxes also affect consumption and investment. And current government spending affects demand directly.

In the two-period overlapping generation model that I have used a few times in the book, the three effects are clear: The consumption of the young depends on taxes this period and expected taxes next period; the consumption of the old depends on their wealth when they become old, thus on their debt holdings, and on the taxes they pay when old; and government spending affects demand directly. In more realistic models, the effects are more intricate:[23]

- By itself, debt is wealth for those who hold it, but it may be partly offset by the expectation of future taxes. Indeed, in the extreme case of infinitely lived, rational forward-looking individuals, for given government spending, any increase in debt is fully offset by an increase in the expected present

---

22. It will be clear what I think of the effects of fiscal policy through a Keynesian or New Keynesian framework: I think of fiscal policy as affecting aggregate demand and output, and of the resulting output gap (the difference between output and potential output) in turn as affecting inflation. An alternative approach to debt dynamics and inflation is the so-called fiscal theory of the price level. The theory treats the price level as an asset price and, using the equation for debt dynamics, determines the price level as the value such that the real value of nominal debt is equal to the present value of primary balances. Smaller primary surpluses in the future lead to a higher price level and a lower value of real debt today. Despite exciting intellectual interactions with John Cochrane, who has written a book on the topic, I remain skeptical of the initial assumption underlying the theory and thus of the theory itself. I believe that, except in times of hyperinflation, the price level does not behave as an asset price but as the aggregate of billions of mostly backward-looking decisions, and that expectations of future primary balances have little effect on the price level today. Only in periods of very high inflation do movements in the price level reflect expectations about current and future fiscal policy. When $r < g$, the present discounted value of future primary balances is infinite, and thus debt can no longer be interpreted as the present discounted value of primary surpluses. What the fiscal theory of the price level may imply in this case is discussed in Cochrane 2022, sec. 6-4.

23. In Blanchard 1985, I constructed a more general index, based on a model where people have finite horizons, showing the respective roles of debt, taxes, and spending on aggregate demand and on the neutral rate.

value of taxes and so has no effect on consumption, a result known as *Ricardian equivalence*. But, in general, because of finite horizons or just myopia, the offset is likely to be much less than one-for-one. And, as we have seen, when $r < g$, higher debt need not require an increase in taxes later on.

• By itself, a decrease in taxes increases income. If the decrease in taxes is expected to extend in the future, the effect is larger. If, instead, it is expected to lead to a reversal and an increase in taxes in the future, the effect is likely to be smaller. Indeed, under the same assumption of infinitely lived, rational forward-looking individuals, and assuming no change in current and expected future government spending, the effect of the decrease in taxes today is fully offset by the expectation of higher taxes in the future, so it has no effect on consumption—which is another way of stating the Ricardian equivalence result. Again, in general, the offset is likely to be much less than one-for-one: Many households may not think about future taxes. Many also may be liquidity constrained and use the decrease in taxes to increase consumption, even if they believe that taxes will increase in the future. In short, decreases in taxes are likely to increase consumption.

• By itself, an increase in government spending mechanically increases aggregate demand. To the extent, however, that it leads people to expect higher taxes in the future, then the direct effect may be partly offset by a decrease in consumption. Again, there is every reason to believe that the offset is limited and that higher government spending increases aggregate demand.

• These are just the first-round effects, and they trigger general equilibrium effects. The textbook example is the Keynesian multiplier, in which the initial effect of a decrease in taxes on income leads to an increase in demand, which leads to an increase in output, which leads to a further increase in income and so on. Again, the strength of the effect depends on many factors, from how many households are liquidity constrained to how open the economy is. The main factor, and the one most relevant for this discussion, is the stance of monetary policy. If a fiscal expansion takes place when output is already at potential, monetary policy is likely to tighten, leading to higher interest rates and thus a smaller effect or even no effect of the fiscal expansion on output. If a fiscal contraction takes place and—as is the case today—monetary policy is constrained by the ELB, it is likely to have a larger adverse effect on output.

The discussion makes clear that the effects of debt, taxes, and spending depend very much on expectations as well as on monetary policy and are likely to vary considerably across space and time. There is no such thing as "a" multiplier. Interestingly, the fiscal consolidation that took place in the wake of the Global Financial Crisis and the ELB constraints on monetary policy have led to what Ramey (2019) has called a renaissance of empirical work on the effects of fiscal policy. Here are what I draw as the major conclusions:

- How much does higher public debt increase aggregate demand and in turn the neutral interest rate, r^*? (Recall that the neutral rate is the rate such that aggregate demand is equal to potential output. Thus, the stronger aggregate demand, the higher the neutral rate.) This is a central question because it determines how much governments can increase debt until r^* and, by implication, r becomes higher than g, and we return to a traditional environment where $r > g$.

Yet it is a difficult question to answer for two reasons. One is that the degree to which the effects of debt are partially offset by the anticipation of future taxes is likely to vary across time and place. For example, as we have seen, in the $(r - g) < 0$ environment, higher debt may not imply future taxes later and thus affect wealth one-for-one. And, empirically, detecting the effects of debt per se on aggregate demand and, by implication, on the neutral interest rate is difficult given that debt moves slowly and many other factors matter more in the short run. Various estimates of the effect of debt on r^* have been given, some based on a calibrated model, some based on regressions. They are summarized in Rachel and Summers 2019 and range from 2 to 4 basis points (bp) for a 1% increase in the ratio of debt to gross domestic product (GDP). Thus, Rachel and Summers argue, the increase in the debt ratio of about 60% since the early 1990s added 1.2% to 2.4% to the neutral rate. Put another way, had public debt ratios not increased, the neutral rate would be even more negative today, lower by another 1.2% to 2.4%.[24] Looking forward rather than backward, another

---

24. For reasons I just discussed, this range must be taken with a grain of salt. But the following back-of-the-envelope computation suggests that it is reasonable. Suppose that the marginal propensity to consume out of wealth is 4%, and because of a partial offset through expected future taxes, only $\alpha \leq 1$ of debt is net wealth. Suppose first that $\alpha = 1$, so debt is fully net wealth. Then, the direct effect on consumption and thus on demand of a 50% increase in debt would be 2%. Suppose α is instead equal

increase in debt—by, say, 50% of GDP—would further increase r^* by 100 bp to 200 bp, substantially reducing the size of the difference between r and g, although probably not changing its sign.

• For our purposes, on the topic of tax and spending multipliers, I draw additional conclusions from the recent research.[25,26,27]

Based on both time-series methods (typically structural vector autoregressions, called VARs) and model simulations (usually New Keynesian dynamic stochastic general equilibrium models, called DSGEs), most estimated multipliers have the expected sign: (plausibly exogenous) increases in taxes decrease output; (plausibly exogenous) decreases in spending decrease output.[28]

Surprisingly, most empirical studies find larger tax multipliers than spending multipliers. In the Ramey survey, spending multipliers range from 0.6 to 1.0.[29] Tax multipliers are, however, typically much larger (in absolute value), ranging from -1.0 to -5.0. This is a surprising number because, in the textbook Keynesian model, the opposite holds: In the first round, taxes affect demand through consumption, thus less than one-for-one, while government spending affects demand directly; the implication is that tax multipliers should be smaller than spending multipliers; this appears not to be the case, whether because of different adjustments of expectations, differences in monetary responses, or other reasons.

---

to 1/2; then the direct effect would be 1%. If the elasticity of aggregate demand with respect to the interest rate is roughly 1, this would imply increases in the neutral rate of 1% to 2%.

25. Ramey (2019) does a nice job of summarizing the recent empirical literature.

26. While the policy discussion is often in terms of deficits, to the extent that multipliers for taxes and spending differ from each other, it is not just the size but the composition of deficits that matter.

27. Multipliers are defined in different ways in different articles, which makes comparisons difficult. Ramey has tried as best as she could, based on the original studies, to compute them as ratios of some discounted or undiscounted sum of GDP responses over time to the corresponding sum of the exogenous change in the fiscal measure.

28. Not everybody is convinced. See, for example, Robert Barro, "Government spending is no free lunch," *Wall Street Journal*, January 22, 2009, in which he expresses the view that multipliers are zero and fiscal policy is not useful.

29. To the extent that spending is investment spending, it affects not just aggregate demand but also aggregate supply. Thus, it may have long-term effects. These effects, however, are hard to detect using time-series methods.

Of direct relevance to the current situation, given the ELB constraint and the high level of debt, is that the multipliers appear larger when the monetary response is more limited (see Leigh et al. 2010). And they appear smaller when debt ratios are high, perhaps because people are more worried that taxes may be increased in the future or that debt may become unsustainable.

In summary, fiscal policy can play a central role in helping keep output at potential. Higher debt increases aggregate demand. Lower taxes or higher spending also do. Multipliers are likely to vary a lot over time and space, but the bulk of the evidence is that they are different from zero, positive for spending, negative for taxes, and that they are stronger when monetary policy does not or cannot react to fiscal policy.

5.4 Putting the Threads Together

Real interest rates are low; debt ratios are high. In this economic environment, what do the arguments developed in the book so far imply for how fiscal policy should be designed? Let me put the various parts of the answer together.

We have seen that the lower the neutral rate, the lower the fiscal costs of debt. Debt dynamics are more favorable; indeed as r^* and by implication r become less than g, governments can run (some) primary deficits while keeping their debt ratio constant.

The lower the neutral rate, the lower the welfare costs of debt. For sufficiently low neutral rates, debt may even have welfare benefits, although it is difficult to pin down the exact rate at which this happens. A reasonable working assumption is that while neutral rates are indeed low, debt still has welfare costs, albeit limited ones.

The lower the neutral rate, the more limited is the room for monetary policy to stabilize output. In particular, if r^* becomes smaller than r_{min}, which is the lowest real rate the central bank can achieve given the effective lower bound, then monetary policy can no longer maintain output at potential. Fiscal support, in the form of deficits, is needed to do so. Even if the effective lower bound is not strictly binding, the closer r^* is to r_{min}, the less room monetary policy has to react to adverse shocks, and the more fiscal support might be needed.

Putting these propositions together: The lower the neutral rate, the smaller the fiscal and welfare costs and the larger the welfare benefits of debt and deficits.

To go one step further, it is useful to think of two extreme approaches to fiscal policy:

• A *pure public finance* approach, focusing on the use of debt to smooth tax distortions or to redistribute income across generations and ignoring the effects of policy on aggregate demand and output. It is widely believed that the levels of debt we observe today are higher than what this approach would suggest. If so, under this approach, debt should be decreased over time, and governments should be running primary surpluses.

• A *pure functional finance* approach—using the terminology introduced by Abba Lerner in 1943—focusing on the macro-stabilization role of fiscal policy and ignoring the effects of policy on debt. Under this approach, if aggregate demand is weak and monetary policy is constrained, then governments should not hesitate to sustain aggregate demand and output and run primary deficits.[30]

We can, then, think of the appropriate fiscal policy as a weighted average of the pure public finance and pure functional finance approaches, with most of the weight on the pure functional finance approach and macro-stabilization when the neutral rate is very low, and most of the weight on the pure public finance approach and debt reduction when the neutral rate is very high.

• Start from a situation where aggregate demand is very weak, reflecting very weak private demand and a given fiscal stance. Suppose that, as a result, the neutral rate is low—indeed, lower than can be achieved by the central bank given the effective lower bound: r^* is less than r_{min} and thus $r = r_{min} < r^*$. As monetary policy cannot set the interest rate low enough to match the neutral rate, output is lower than potential. Then, priority must be given to macro-stabilization and an increase in the budget deficit so as to return output to potential.

---

30. Despite numerous discussions, I have found it difficult to know exactly what Modern Monetary Theory (MMT) stands for. I interpret as one of its main tenets that fiscal policy, rather than monetary policy, should be used for macroeconomic stabilization. If so, I do share that view when the neutral rate is very low and monetary policy cannot be used, but not when the neutral rate is higher.

How large should the increase in deficits be? At a minimum, it should be enough to bring r^* back up to r_{min}. By doing so, it brings output back to potential, and the central bank can set the policy rate just equal to the neutral rate: $r = r_{min} = r^*$. This, however, leaves no room for monetary policy to react to further adverse shocks, as the effective lower bound is still strictly binding. Thus, what fiscal policy should do is aim for a higher value of r^*—say, $r^* = r_{min} + x$—to give some room to monetary policy. How large x should be depends on the trade-off between giving more room to monetary policy versus increasing the costs of debt.

Implementation could take various forms. The government could be in the lead and choose the size of the deficit. It would lead to overheating, causing the central bank to respond by increasing r in line with r^*. Or it could take the form of a coordinated fiscal expansion/monetary contraction, with the government increasing demand and the central bank increasing the interest rate, so as to achieve potential output at the desired value of the neutral rate r^*.

What would obviously be the wrong fiscal policy would be to give, in this context, priority to the pure public finance approach and embark on a fiscal consolidation in order to decrease debt. Given the assumption that, in this case, monetary policy is constrained by the effective lower bound, the effect would be a decrease in output. It would lead to a large welfare cost from lower output and only a small welfare gain in terms of lower debt (more on this when discussing the shift to fiscal austerity in the wake of the Global Financial Crisis in chapter 6). The box, "The effects on debt and output from fiscal austerity when the effective lower bound is binding," gives a sense of what the outcome for debt and output might be if such a policy were indeed to be pursued.

Note an important implication: If such a policy was followed, we should never observe rates lower than $r_{min} + x$. In effect, fiscal policy would set a floor for the neutral rate, standing ready to increase deficits if the neutral rate decreased below $r_{min} + x$.

• Now, assume that private demand becomes stronger. How should fiscal policy adjust?

The same logic as the one used above suggests that, if private demand becomes stronger, the policy adjustment should take the form of delivering both some increase in the room for monetary policy and some reduction in the deficit. In other words, the increase in private demand should be partly offset by a decrease in the deficit so as to lead to a smaller increase in aggregate demand than in private demand. And this net increase in aggregate demand should itself be offset by a monetary contraction, an increase in the policy rate, in order to maintain demand and output at potential. The outcome should be a smaller deficit, a higher neutral rate, and more room for monetary policy. Again, implementation of this combination of fiscal and monetary consolidation can take the form of fiscal policy in the lead and monetary policy reacting to avoid overheating and to keep output at potential, or of coordination between the two in reaction to the movements in private demand. (Another issue related to coordination between fiscal and monetary policy—namely, the coordination of decisions affecting the average maturity of the debt of the consolidated government—is explained in the box below.)

As private demand increases further, the marginal benefit of increased room for monetary policy becomes smaller, and the marginal cost of debt becomes larger. This implies that the fiscal offset to private demand should become stronger. Indeed, when private demand becomes very strong and monetary policy has sufficient room to offset most adverse shocks, including fiscal consolidation, then the government can focus on the pure public finance approach and run the surpluses it deems appropriate to reduce the debt over time, leaving monetary policy fully in charge of macro-stabilization.

The effects on debt and output from fiscal austerity when the effective lower bound is binding

The following quantitative example gives a sense of the trade-off between the effects of a fiscal consolidation on the debt ratio and on output when monetary policy cannot decrease the policy rate:

• Assume that the debt ratio is 100%, that $(r-g)/(1+g) = -3\%$, and that the primary deficit is initially 3%, so the debt ratio is constant.

• Assume that, in order to decrease the debt ratio, the government increases taxes by 1% of GDP. Given the effective lower bound, the resulting decrease in demand cannot be offset by the central bank. Use a small value of the multiplier—say, 1.0 (given the evidence presented in section 5.3, this is a lower bound, and using a higher value would strengthen the conclusion)—so the decrease in output as a result of the tax increase is 1%.

- Assume an automatic stabilizer value of 0.5, so the effect of a decrease in GDP of 1% leads to a decrease in revenues of 0.5% of GDP; the net increase in taxes, and thus the improvement in the primary balance, is 0.5% of GDP.

- Suppose the government maintains this increase in taxes for five years in a row. Then, at the end of five years, the debt ratio has decreased from 100% to approximately 97.5%. If the worry was that debt was too high and exposed the country to excessive interest rate risk, note how this long period of fiscal austerity and lower output does little to decrease the interest burden if r^* were to increase in the future by, say, 3%: Debt service as a ratio to GDP would increase by 2.92% instead of 3%. At the same time, the welfare cost of 1% lower output, and the associated higher unemployment for five years, is large.

- The trade-off could be even worse if we used the larger multipliers we saw in section 5.3. It would also be worse if hysteresis was at work and if keeping output below potential for an extended period of time led to a decrease in potential output.[a] Indeed, there may be no trade-off at all: If hysteresis is sufficiently strong, fiscal austerity may lead to a larger proportional decrease in output than in debt and thus to a permanent increase in the debt ratio. Going beyond economic effects, it would also be worse if a long period of unemployment above the natural rate led to political unrest and the risk of electing a populist government.

- Clearly, if debt could be reduced quickly to 50% at little cost in output, this would make a substantive difference if and when the interest rate increased, but such a decrease is outside the realm of what can be realistically achieved, short of debt cancellation—which is not in the cards and, as I have argued in chapter 4, is simply not needed today.

---

a. See DeLong and Summers 2012.

The tug of war between QE and Treasury debt management

Apart from the basic issue of coordination between fiscal and monetary policy, another coordination issue arises in the determination of the average maturity of the debt held by outside investors. As interest rates decreased in the past, Treasuries increased the average maturity of the public debt so as to lock in the low rates and decrease the risks of a sudden increase in short-term interest rates on interest payments. In parallel, as central banks hit the effective lower bound on the policy rate and could not decrease it further, they embarked on purchases of government (and other) securities, a policy known as quantitative easing (QE) so as to decrease the interest rate on longer maturity bonds. In doing so, they bought long maturity government bonds and issued in exchange interest-paying, zero maturity, central bank reserves.

The tension between the two sets of actions is obvious, however. If we think of the debt of the consolidated government (Treasury plus central bank), the actions of the Treasury increased maturity while the actions of the central bank reduced it. The net result, in terms of the maturity of the debt held by private investors, has in many cases been roughly a wash. Take, for example, what happened during the financial crisis in the United States. Between December 2007 and July 2014, the duration of debt of the federal government increased from 3.9 to 4.6 years. But the duration of the consolidated government debt (thus including zero maturity, interest-paying central bank reserves) held by private investors actually *decreased* from 4.1 to 3.8 years (Greenwood et al. 2014).

Was it mostly a wash, a waste of two offsetting operations? Not completely, because as a result of both sets of operations, consolidated government debt included a larger proportion of interest-paying central bank reserves, and, in contrast to government bonds, central bank reserves are not runnable, thus decreasing the risk of a run on debt. Still, it is the case that the result of these operations is that the government remains more exposed to interest rate risk than it would want.

The issues, looking forward, are twofold. As aggregate demand increases, should central banks phase out quantitative easing and let the Treasury manage the maturity of the debt? Indeed, one can see the choice of a higher value of r^* as allowing the central bank to rely more on the policy rate and phase out its QE operations faster, letting the Treasury be in charge of debt management and avoiding the need for coordination. And, if central banks decide to continue to rely on QE and have large balance sheets, even as policy rates become positive again, how should these be coordinated with Treasuries?[a]

---

a. For further discussion, see Masuch 2021.

That this characterization of policy is only a first pass is obvious. While the principles are clear, much more formalization and quantitative work is needed to make these recommendations operational.[31] It also raises a number of issues, to which I now turn.

---

31. For a related, more analytical approach to the design of fiscal policy and the role of secular stagnation and the ELB, see Mian, Straub, and Sufi 2021a.

Will Fiscal Policy Actually Work? Revisiting Multipliers

If deficits lead to an increase in debt ratios starting from already high levels, could it be that they will not have the desired effect on aggregate demand?[32] Can we be sure that multipliers will have the right sign? Could a fiscal expansion in the current context be contractionary, or could a fiscal contraction be expansionary? This argument, which some used as the basis for *expansionary fiscal austerity* after the Global Financial Crisis, was that it would reassure investors that the government was committed to keeping debt sustainable, and that increased investors' confidence would lead in turn to a large decrease in spreads and to a decrease in interest rates, not just for the government but for the private sector as well, all leading to an increase in aggregate demand.[33] The argument cannot be rejected out of hand, and there are indeed cases in history where this confidence effect was probably at work.[34] There is now wide agreement that, even if this effect was partly at work in 2009 and 2010, it was not sufficient, and fiscal austerity was unambiguously contractionary during that period.[35] (I have more to say on this episode in the chapter 6.) In the current context, this argument, which I expect to come back soon in the conversation, also does not appear relevant. The spreads are very low already (indicating that investors are not worried about debt sustainability) and thus cannot decrease much.

What Is the Inflation Target?

The value of the real safe rate at the effective lower bound (which is a bound on the nominal rate, not on the real rate), r_{min}, depends one-for-one on expected inflation. The higher expected inflation, the lower the real safe rate at the effective lower bound, and thus the less need for fiscal deficits to sustain output. This raises the old issue of the right inflation target. The issue of the optimal rate of inflation has been long debated, but its implication for fiscal policy—namely, the need to run deficits when the ELB is binding—has typically not been taken into account. That a higher inflation rate would

---

32. Recall that primary deficits, if not too large, may be consistent with a stable or even with a decreasing debt ratio. But if private demand is so depressed that it requires large primary deficits, debt may go up in spite of very low rates.

33. See, for example, Alesina and Ardagna 2009.

34. See Giavazzi and Pagano 1990, and my discussion of them in Blanchard 1990.

35. See, for example, Blanchard and Leigh 2013.

be desirable has led to proposals for engineering a strong fiscal expansion, together with monetary policy keeping r below r^* for some time, so as to generate overheating and an increase in the inflation rate above the current target, perhaps leading to an upward revision of the target.[36] The stimulus plan passed during President Joe Biden's administration, together with a dovish attitude by the Fed, can be seen as indeed intentionally overheating the economy, with the goal of creating, at least temporarily, higher inflation. The Fed, however, has not revised its target inflation up and, so far, gives no indication of doing so (more on this in chapter 6, when discussing the effects of the Biden administration stimulus).[37]

What If Secular Stagnation Becomes Worse?

What if private demand remains so weak that, despite the central bank remaining at the ELB, the required primary deficits are so large that the debt ratio steadily increases, putting into question debt sustainability? The question is clearly relevant for Japan and its already very high debt ratios (more on this in chapter 6, when discussing Japanese fiscal policy over the last 30 years and its future prospects) and raises the issue of whether there are alternatives to fiscal deficits to sustain aggregate demand.

Some researchers have suggested relying on the Keynesian *balanced budget multiplier*—that is, on an equal increase in spending and in taxes. The logic of the argument is that to the extent that taxes work through consumption, and given that the marginal propensity to consume is less than one, they have a less than one-for-one effect on demand, whereas spending affects demand directly and one-for-one. Although this works in the textbooks, the empirical evidence I discussed earlier suggests that tax multipliers are actually *larger* than spending multipliers, and if so, such a balanced budget increase would most likely have perverse effects.

A more promising way is to focus on the determinants of r^*, and whether some of these determinants can be affected by policy. The analysis of the factors behind low r^* suggest a number of leads.

---

36. See, for example, Michau 2020. See also Ubide 2017.
37. This paragraph is about target and thus expected inflation. Unexpected inflation (unexpected at the time the investors bought the bonds) is a different animal. As we are seeing in the United States at the time of writing, it can lead to a reduction in the real value of debt. But, by its very nature of being unexpected, it cannot be a sustained policy.

On the investment side, it might be that some green public investment triggers a large increase in related private investment and thus a potentially large increase in demand (and in supply later on). The evidence on the spillover effects of green investment is limited but suggestive. A study by the Council of Economic Advisers (2016) concluded that the $46 billion allocated in the American Recovery and Reinvestment Act (ARRA) package passed in the United States in 2009 led to more than $150 billion in private and non federal public investment, thus a high multiplier. Another study (Aldy 2013) estimates that the clean energy manufacturing tax credit included in the same ARRA package, with a total tax expenditure cap of $2.3 billion, supported co-investment of $5.4 billion. A third study (Springel 2021), based on Norwegian data, finds that one dollar invested in charging stations led to four dollars in increased purchases of electric vehicles. Batini et al. (2021), using a structural VAR approach, conclude that the multipliers associated with spending on renewable and fossil fuel energy investment range from 1.1 to 1.5.[38],[39]

On the saving side, Mian, Straub, and Sufi (2021b) have argued that because the rich save proportionately more than the poor, increasing inequality in the United States since the early 1980s has contributed to higher saving and to the decrease in r^*. Realistically, however, the decrease in inequality that would lead to significantly less saving is out of reach. I believe that in some countries, one of the most promising leads is to focus on precautionary saving. The provision of more social insurance—say, an extension of the Affordable Care Act (also known as Obamacare) or the provision of "Medicare for all" in the United States—would be good on its own, but presumably it would also lead to less precautionary saving, an increase in private demand, and a lower need for budget deficits. In any case, if secular stagnation continues to dominate, these and other directions will have to be explored.

---

38. A theme running through the various studies is the importance of accompanying these measures with a clear path for the carbon price. Some investments, such as the carbon capture and storage project, again in the ARRA, failed because of low carbon prices later.

39. A related dimension, looking upstream, is the evidence on knowledge spillovers, measured by patent citations. They appear substantially higher for low-carbon technologies than for high-carbon technologies, probably because of their novelty relative to older technologies (see Dechezleprêtre, Martin, and Mohnen 2017).

6 Fiscal Policy in Action

The chapter looks at three recent episodes where, for better or for worse, fiscal policy played or is playing a major role. The purpose is not to review them in full, which would take another book, but to show and discuss fiscal policy choices in the light of the analysis so far.

To caricature just a bit, the three episodes can be thought of "too little," "just right," and "too much."

Too little? The first section looks at the period of "fiscal austerity" that took place in the wake of the Global Financial Crisis (GFC). After the large initial increase in debt resulting from the crisis, the focus quickly turned to debt reduction. This was particularly true in the European Union (EU), which embarked on strong fiscal consolidation. Today, there is fairly wide agreement that, at least in Europe, the fiscal consolidation was too strong and relied too much on the traditional view of debt, both by markets and by policymakers, and came at a substantial output cost.

Just right? The second section looks at the Japanese economy over the last three decades. Japan experienced the effective lower bound (ELB) constraint starting in the mid-1990s, earlier than either the United States or Europe, and has remained close to it ever since. Japanese macroeconomic policy is often characterized as a failure, with the central bank unable to achieve its inflation target, a low growth rate, and debt ratios steadily rising to reach more than 170% for net debt and 250% for gross debt. I think it should be seen instead as a qualified success, with the use of aggressive fiscal and monetary policies to compensate for very weak private demand: Output has remained close to potential. Growth is low, but mostly because of demographics, not because of debt. Inflation is low, lower than the target, but this is not a major failure. Looking forward, however, there are reasons to worry. The debt ratios are very high. So far, investors do not mind, and 10-year nominal rates are close to zero. But can the buildup of debt continue? What happens if interest rates increase? Are there alternatives?

Too much? The third section looks at the effects of the American Rescue Plan, the stimulus program put in place by President Joe Biden's administration in early 2021. In 2020, the focus of fiscal policy had been protection, of both households and firms. In early 2021, the goal partially shifted from protection to sustaining the recovery. The size of the program was extremely large relative to apparent output gap. The strategy (intentional or not) was in effect twofold. For the Treasury, it was to strongly increase aggregate demand and thus achieve both higher output and a higher neutral rate, so as to relax the ELB constraint. And for the Federal Reserve, the goal was to delay adjustment of the policy rate to the neutral rate, allow for some overheating, and generate slightly higher inflation in the process. To a number of observers, the size of the program appeared too large, leading to worries about overheating and excessive inflation. This chapter takes stock of where things are at the time of writing.

6.1   Fiscal Austerity in the Wake of the GFC

The Global Financial Crisis started in earnest in the fall of 2008. For the remainder of 2008 and much of 2009, the reaction of governments was to spend whatever appeared needed, without worrying much about debt. The response was strongest in the United States, where the American Recovery and Reinvestment Act (ARRA), passed in February 2009, committed to additional spending and tax measures adding to $830 billion, or 5.9% of gross domestic product (GDP). The 2009 primary balance was equal to −11.2% of GDP, up from −4.6% in 2008. The European Economic Recovery Plan (EERP), adopted in November 2008, recommended that governments take measures adding to 200 billion euros for the European Union as a whole, or 1.5% of EU GDP. The euro area 2009 primary balance was −3.8%, up from 0.4% in 2008. Japan passed a number of programs as the crisis got worse, for a total of 29 trillion yen in additional measures, or 5.8% of GDP. Japan's primary deficit for 2009 was −9.3%, up from −3.8% in 2008.[1]

As a result, at the end of 2009 the (net) debt ratio stood at 63% for the United States, up 11% compared to the end of 2008; it stood at 62% for

---

1. IMF Fiscal Monitor, Methodological and Statistical Appendix, 2017.

the euro area, up 8%; and it was 96% for Japan, up 11.3%. In addition to the increase in official debt, there was a large increase in contingent liabilities, as governments embarked on off-balance sheet operations, such as the Troubled Asset Relief Program (TARP), passed in the United States at the end of 2008, authorizing the purchase or the insurance of assets up to $700 billion.

In parallel, central banks decreased rates down to or close to the zero lower bound. In the United States, the federal funds rate decreased from 2.0% in August 2008 to 0.1% by December. In Europe, the euro discount rate decreased from 5.25% in September of 2008 to 1.75% by March 2009. In Japan, which was already de facto at the ELB before the crisis, the policy rate was reduced from 0.50% in September to 0.1% by the end of the year.

From the start, governments had insisted on the need for "timely, targeted, and temporary" fiscal measures. By the end of 2009, as economies appeared to slowly recover, the focus turned to debt consolidation. To get a sense of the shift in emphasis, I examined communiqués from the Group of Twenty (G20) and the executive summaries of the International Monetary Fund (IMF) Fiscal Monitor. I used a grading system from +2 to −2: A focus on output stabilization rather than debt reduction was graded +2; a focus on debt reduction rather than output stabilization was graded −2. More balanced statements were graded between +2 and −2. The exercise is obviously subjective (although not obviously less reliable than an artificial intelligence (AI) approach to the same issue) but turns out to be highly suggestive.[2]

The results are presented in figure 6.1. After expressing strong support for output stabilization until early 2010, the G20 communiqués took a sharp turn and refocused nearly exclusively on the need to decrease debt, despite the fact that central banks were still at or very close to their effective lower bound. The IMF was more dovish, also shifting in 2010 to an emphasis on debt reduction but, as the recovery sputtered, putting more weight on output stabilization from 2011 on.

The shift to a focus on debt reduction was particularly strong in the European Union. Precrisis, in June 2008, the assessment of the European Union

---

2. Thanks to Michael Kister for taking the first pass at the text. This material also comes with the warning that the author is both judge and party in the exercise, having been the chief economist of the IMF during that period, and the analyst in this book today.

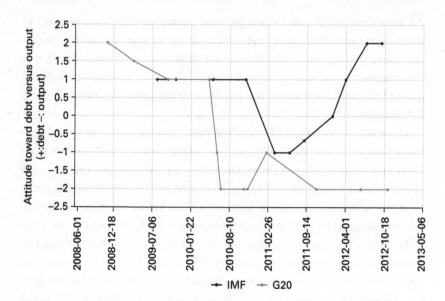

Figure 6.1
Attitude toward debt reduction versus output stabilization, G20 and IMF.
Source: G20 communiqués and IMF Fiscal Monitor executive summaries, different years.

Commission Public Finance reports had been that most countries satisfied the Maastricht criteria. In 2009, the Commission expressed support for the EERP but insisted on the "temporary" aspect of the stimulus.

In 2010, the Commission decided that there would be no suspension of the EU fiscal rules and shifted the focus to an "exit strategy." Given the increase in debt, it put most countries in the "corrective arm" of the Stability and Growth Pact and started the Excessive Deficit Procedure (EDP), requiring countries to return to the medium-term objective for debt within a horizon of two to three years. It invoked increasing spreads and thus the need to reassure markets, but the message was more general, applying to all member countries, including those whose spread had not increased. The message was unambiguous.

> In view of the challenges, the planned pace of the fiscal consolidation should be ambitious, and will have to go well beyond the benchmark of 0.5% of GDP per annum in structural terms in most Member States. (EU commission Public Finances in EMU, 2010, p. 3)

In 2011, despite the slowing recovery, and the fact that the European Central Bank (ECB) was still close to the effective lower bound, the

Commission doubled down, insisting on the need not just to stabilize debt ratios but to decrease them.

> The issue of sustainability has emerged as the key concern in the immediate postcrisis years. Soaring deficits and off-balance-sheet operations to support the financial sector have led to a large increase in debt for nearly all European Union countries. Despite the fact that a return of GDP growth, a gradual withdrawal of the temporary support measures, and the start of consolidation is starting to reduce deficits, debt is still expected to continue increasing for the next year or so in most cases. Once it has reached its peak, the issue is not over. It will not be sufficient to stem the increase; rather, additional consolidation measures will be required to reduce it from its new level, not least because population aging is due to have an increasingly negative effect on the public finances and put pressure on their sustainability in coming decades. (EU commission Public Finances in EMU, 2011, p. ix)

The Commission proposed changes in the rules, which in effect made the rules tougher. It added expenditure benchmarks, introduced numerical criteria for the minimal speed of debt-ratio adjustment—namely, 1/20th of the difference between the debt ratio and 60%.

In 2012, the Commission tripled down, despite negative growth of −0.8% (year on year) for the euro area.

> The significant increase in debt ratios seen since the start of the crisis alongside the still sizable deficits mean that there is little scope for many Member States to ease off the fiscal tightening, despite the extra pressure that this might put on already faltering growth. Amid the debate about how best to continue to respond to the crisis, concerns have been raised that further fiscal consolidation amid weak growth prospects may have self-defeating effects on debt ratios. Part III presents a detailed analysis that highlights how such effects may arise but concludes that such cases are rather theoretical and anyhow short-lived under reasonable economic assumptions. (European Commission Report on Public Finances in EMU, 2012, p. xi)

What is interesting in the Commission's assessment is that the concern is not about growth per se but about whether lower growth will make debt reduction self-defeating.

In 2013, growth was still negative at −0.2%. "Whatever it takes," announced by Mario Draghi in July 2012, had considerably reduced the spreads on sovereign bonds, especially for Portugal, Italy, and Ireland, but there still was no change in the message: Admittedly, "deleveraging of the public sector" was tough and affected output, but it was necessary to continue fiscal consolidation.

Improvements in the financial conditions have had limited impact on the real economy so far. Economic activity disappointed in the second half of 2012 and turned out weaker than expected in the first quarter of 2013. This was due to two interrelated set of factors. First, because of persistent weaknesses in the banking sector, the improvement in the financial markets' situation has not yet fed in the credit growth. . . . Second, the process of deleveraging of the private and the public sector is still ongoing in many economies, and this weighs on aggregate demand. In particular, domestic demand remains muted due to high unemployment and as a result of persistent uncertainty amongst households and enterprises regarding the future economic outlook and the development of the debt crisis. At the same time, given the remaining fiscal sustainability concerns, governments in many Member States have to continue the necessary fiscal retrenchment. (European Commission Report on Public Finances in EMU, 2013, p. 13)

How costly, in terms of output, was fiscal austerity? Counterfactuals are not available, but what can be done is to look at the cross-country evidence. Simple bivariate graphs have obvious limits and show correlation rather than causality, but they are suggestive. Figure 6.2 plots the change in the output gap between 2014 and 2008 against the change in the cyclically adjusted primary balance during the same period, both as ratios to GDP, for the 27 advanced economies for which the data is available. There is a clear significant and negative relation between the two. The regression coefficient, −0.48, implies that a 1% higher cyclically adjusted primary surplus was associated with a worsening of the output gap of about 0.5%, both as ratios to GDP. The results are similar when only European Union members are included (the regression coefficient is −0.32).[3,4]

In summary: In the wake of the global financial crisis, and while central banks were still at or close to the ELB, policymakers put too much weight on debt reduction relative to output stabilization. Put another way, it was

---

3. In both cases, Greece is excluded from the graph and the regression. It is an extreme outlier because the change in the primary balance was equal to 13.5% of GDP, and the output gap worsened by 17% of GDP. Including Greece would lead to a much stronger statistical relation but would be largely determined by one data point. 4. One may also question (as I have elsewhere) the construction of output gaps. Using the unemployment rate instead of the output gap also yields a strong positive relation between the change in the unemployment rate and the change in the primary balance. The coefficient of the corresponding regression, for the sample of advanced economies, is 0.19. An increase in the primary balance of 1% is associated with an increase in the unemployment rate of 0.19%.

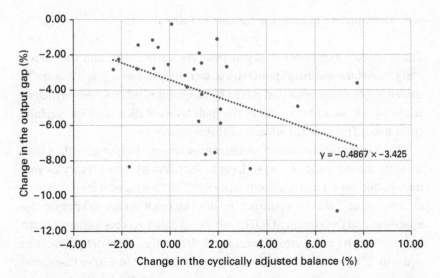

Figure 6.2
Output gap versus change in cyclically adjusted primary balance.
Sources: World Economic Outlook data for output gap, IMP Fiscal Monitor data for cyclically adjusted primary balance.

a case of too little fiscal support. The costs of high debt were perceived to be very high—higher than they truly were—and the multipliers were underestimated, leading to an underestimate of the output costs of fiscal consolidation.[5,6,7]

---

5. In work with Daniel Leigh (Blanchard and Leigh 2013), we showed that forecast errors for growth were correlated with the size of the planned fiscal adjustment. Forecast errors were more negative the larger the size of the planned adjustment. As unbiased forecasts should lead to zero correlation of the forecast errors with variables in the information set at the time of the forecast, the natural interpretation is that policymakers systematically underestimated the adverse effect of fiscal consolidation on growth.

6. This assessment is even shared by some of the architects of the policy. See, for example, the very honest account by Buti 2021.

7. In his book, Marco Buti (2021) draws an interesting contrast between the behavior of the EU in the financial crisis and the Covid crisis. In the first one, a major theme was moral hazard. Countries in the South were seen as having misbehaved and being likely to do so again if not restrained. In the Covid crisis, the problem is clearly not due to misbehavior and has affected countries in the North as well as in the South. This has contributed to the adoption of a more flexible view.

6.2   The Japanese Experience: Success or Failure?

The economic experience of Japan since the early 1990s, and the under-lying monetary and fiscal policies, are seen by some as a major failure.[8] I shall make the argument that it is in fact a qualified success.[9] Nevertheless, the implications and the risks of the high levels of debt must be carefully considered. These are the themes of this section.

The case for failure appears straightforward: poor output growth, a con-sistently missed inflation target, large budget deficits, and a legacy of very high public debt. Japan's growth since 1992 has averaged 0.8% relative to an average of 2.0% for countries in the Organisation for Economic Co-operation and Development (OECD).[10] Fiscal policy has been characterized by large deficits and a steady increase in debt ratios, with net public debt equal to 171% of GDP in 2020 and gross debt equal to 250%. Consumer Price Index (CPI) inflation has run at an average of 0.3%, much lower than the target of 2%.

The case is, however, weaker than it seems.

Lower Japanese growth reflects mostly lower population growth (0% since 1995) and, by implication, lower labor force growth (0.1%).[11] Produc-tivity growth measured as output per worker has been 0.6%, which is similar to the 0.5% for the EU19 (the 19 advanced economy members of the Euro-pean Union before the last extension), although lower than the 1.6% for the United States. Productivity growth measured as output per hour has been 1.3%, which is higher than the EU19 1.0% but again lower than the US 1.7%.

The unemployment rate has remained low, only slightly exceeding 5% twice, first in 2001 after a steady increase in response to the crash of the asset bubble (which happened 10 years earlier), then during the Global Financial Crisis in 2009, but returning over time to 2.8% in 2021, close to its value of 2.1% in 1990.

---

8. For a detailed analysis of the evolution of the Japanese economy since 1990, see Ito and Hoshi 2020.
9. The statement is intentionally provocative and refers only to the macro-stabilization task of economic policy. One might well argue that the successive governments fell short in not implementing a number of needed structural reforms.
10. While the bursting of the asset bubble took place in 1990, growth remained strong in 1990 and 1991. Thus the choice of 1992 as a starting date.
11. The choice of the initial date is determined by data constraints when comparing with the European Union.

Inflation has remained substantially lower than the target of 2%, alternating periods of small inflation and small deflation around an average of 0.3% for CPI inflation since 1992. How should this be interpreted? The Phillips curve relation implies that, if expectations are stable, an inflation rate lower than the expected inflation rate indicates that unemployment is above the natural rate and that there is a negative output gap. Evidence on inflation expectations suggests, however, that inflation expectations have remained lower than the target, around 1% on average, but are still not quite as low as actual inflation (Maruyama and Suganuma 2019). This suggests that, on average, output has remained below, but close to, potential.

It is true, though, that this was accompanied by a steady string of large deficits and a large increase in public debt, to which I now turn.

There are at least two reasons why governments run budget deficits. The first is unintentional: Faced with adverse shocks or adverse trends, governments are unable to raise sufficient revenues to cover public spending. The other is intentional: Faced with weak private demand, governments run deficits to sustain demand and output (automatic stabilizers are a mix of the two). The question is, which one of the two best characterizes Japanese fiscal policy since 1990.

The evolution of primary deficits, as ratios to GDP, in Japan since 1990 is shown in figure 6.3.

It makes clear that, in the 1990s, the first reason played a central role. The sharp shift from a primary surplus of 3% in 1990 to a primary deficit close to 10% in 1998 was essentially due to the dramatic decrease in growth (from 4.3% in the 1980s to 1.3% in the 1990s) following the bursting of the asset bubble. But aging has also had an important and adverse role on public finances through most of the period: The proportion of people age 65 and older has doubled, reaching 30% in 2021, leading to steadily higher health and retirement spending pressure. Successive governments have found it hard to sufficiently increase taxes in parallel, leading to unintentional deficits and attempts by governments to reduce them.

At the same time, governments have been aware of the need to sustain demand and output in the face of weak private demand and of the macroeconomic risks in reducing deficits.

This tension between the two goals has led to somewhat schizophrenic but not unusual outcomes. In the 1990s, ambivalence about whether to limit the increase in debt or sustain demand led to stop-and-go policies: A large expansion in 1995 was followed by contraction in 1996

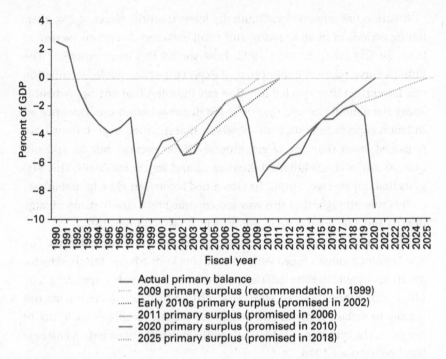

Figure 6.3
Japan primary balance.
Source: Courtesy of Takeshi Tashiro.

and 1997 (Posen 2013). From 2000 on, as shown in figure 6.3, governments started to set zero primary balance targets 10 years out, implying a steady reduction in deficits, of the order of 0.6% to 0.8% per year over the following 10 years, independent of the need for demand support. These announced target paths were actually more than words: Figure 6.3 shows that, leaving aside the adverse shocks from the Global Financial Crisis and the Covid crisis, each of which led to a large increase in deficits, successive governments were actually staying close to their announced paths. But those two crises led to much larger deficits and a reset of the adjustment from large initial deficit ratios.

The following statement by Prime Minister Shinzo Abe in 2017 is a good example of how recent governments perceive the balance between the desirability of reducing debt and the need for macro-stabilization:[12]

---

12. Prime Minister Shinzo Abe's remarks to the Committee on Budget, the House of Councillors, March 1, 2017.

If we were to cut the budget for the next fiscal year in half, the primary balance would turn into surplus. The moment it turns into surplus, the Japanese economy will be as if it is dead, and from the following year onwards, disastrous things will happen.

The current government of Japan has made clear that there may be a need to run deficits to sustain demand if needed, together with the fact that with $(r - g) \leq 0$, this allows for the government to run some deficits while allowing the debt ratio to stabilize or even to decrease. The following quote from the current vice minister of finance states it as follows:[13]

In order to achieve fiscal soundness, the single year deficits must be reduced more than sufficiently (or, to be precise, at least to within"the surplus of the growth rate minus the interest rate") during the interest rate bonus period. [Note: the period during which g exceeds r is called the bonus period.] If this is done, further deterioration of public finances can be avoided somehow. This is the bottom line (minimum goal) and the royal road that Japan should aim for.

The tension between sustaining demand and decreasing debt is still there. Whether the statement in the quote above is consistent with the promise to go back to primary balance by 2025, starting from a primary deficit of 8.4% in 2020, and with the Bank of Japan (BOJ) still at the effective lower bound, is doubtful. Indeed, IMF forecasts of the Japanese primary balance in 2025 (which includes social security funds) is −2.0%.

Overall, one can see the combination of fiscal and monetary policy—that is, large (partly unintentional, partly intentional) deficits, on the one hand, and monetary policy at the ELB, on the other—as having maintained output in Japan close to potential in the face of chronically low private demand.[14] This is the sense in which Japan can be considered a qualified success (again, it is hard to know what the counterfactual would have been).

Still, deficits have been so large that they have much more than compensated for the favorable debt dynamics coming from $(r - g) < 0$; gross debt ratios have increased from 63% in 1990 to a forecast of 250% by the end of 2021, and net debt ratios have increased from 19% in 1990 to a forecast 171% by the end of 2021. This raises three sets of questions.

---

13. Koji Yano, *Bungeishunju*, November 2021.
14. One may question whether fiscal policy actually made a difference (i.e., it may depend on what the multipliers were in Japan during that time). Goode, Liu, and Nguyen (2021) [56], looking at Japan from 1980 to 2019, conclude that spending multipliers were large, especially when the ELB was binding.

What deficits can Japan run to sustain output while preventing the debt ratio from increasing further?

To answer this question, a rough computation, based on the basic equation for debt dynamics, is useful. Five-year nominal rates are equal to -0.1%; five-year forecasts of inflation are 1.0% annually; five-year forecasts of growth, leaving out the high growth rate from the recovery from Covid in 2022, are 0.8% annually.[15] The net debt ratio is 171%. This implies that $(r-g)b$ is equal to $(-0.1\% -1.0\% -0.8\%) * 171\%$, so -3.2%. This implies that the Japanese government can, in expected value, run a primary deficit of 3.2% and stabilize the debt ratio.

Is it enough to get and keep output at potential? For this, one needs a macro model, and assumptions about the strength of private demand post-Covid, but the answer would appear to be yes: IMF forecasts for 2025 are that, with primary deficit ratios of 2%, the unemployment rate will be 2.3%, which is close to the natural rate. Under those assumptions, the IMF forecasts a slight decline in the net debt ratio down to 169% from 171% in 2021.

This suggests that, under current forecasts, and despite very high debt, Japan does not face a debt sustainability problem. A theme of chapter 4 on debt sustainability was, however, that a full assessment required to explore outcomes not just under the point forecasts, but taking into account the uncertainty and thus the distributions of the various variables involved. So, this triggers the next question.

What would happen if interest rates increased substantially?

All the variables affecting debt dynamics are uncertain, from the primary balance needed if Covid turns out to be persistent, to the underlying growth rate of the economy, and so on. Clearly, the main worry (from the point of view of debt sustainability) is that real interest rates might increase substantially and make it difficult to avoid a debt explosion. To discuss the issue, we can again draw on the discussion of debt sustainability in chapter 4.[16]

How much one should worry about interest rate increases depends first on the average maturity of the public debt. The longer the maturity of the

---

15. The choice of the five-year horizon is because the IMF forecasts only extend five years out.

16. I also draw on Blanchard and Tashiro 2019.

government debt, the less the government budget constraint is affected by a temporary increase in interest rates and the more time the government has to adjust to a permanent increase. The average maturity of public debt is 8.2 years.[17] As a result of massive quantitative easing (QE), however, 45% of the debt is now held by the Bank of Japan, which in turn has issued zero-maturity central bank reserves for the corresponding amount. Thus, the average maturity of the debt of the consolidated Japanese government (Treasury and Bank of Japan) is roughly half of the average maturity of government debt. This is substantially shorter and exposes the Japanese government to a substantial amount of interest risk.

The next question is thus: *Why might interest rates increase and what does it imply?*

The first possibility is a sunspot/sudden stop increase. We have just seen that, absent an increase in interest rates, Japanese debt appears sustainable. But, as we discussed in chapter 4, if investors become worried and require a spread to hold Japan government bonds (JGBs), then their worries can be self-fulfilling. For example, an increase in the real rate from −1.1% to, say, 2% would require the Japanese government to increase its primary balance by 5.3% of GDP. It might not be able to do so, both because of the catastrophic output effects and political constraints on how much taxes can be increased or spending can be cut. Can the BOJ eliminate that risk? The answer is probably yes. First, JBGs have a very stable investor base: Only 13% of government debt is held by foreign investors. Traditionally, Japanese investors have been more stable. Second, the BOJ is now the major holder of JBGs and would play the role of a stable investor, unwilling to sell with other investors and being willing to buy when others sell. Indeed, it may not have to buy on a very large scale, so a commitment by the BOJ to maintain low spreads is credible.

The second possibility is an increase in Japan's private demand, leading to an increase in r^*, given fiscal policy. Were fiscal policy to remain unchanged, the result would indeed be an increase in r as well, if the BOJ sets the policy rate equal to the neutral rate. But the problem in this case has a natural solution, which follows the conclusions reached in chapter 5. As aggregate demand increases, the government can reduce its deficit, thus

17. IMF Fiscal Monitor, October 2021, table A23.

offsetting, at least in part, the increase in private demand and thus limiting the increase in r^* and, in turn, the required increase in r.[18]

Let me again go through a blunt computation. Start from a stable debt ratio and the assumption that $r = r^* = 0\%$. Suppose that with unchanged fiscal policy, private demand increases by 2% of GDP and, assuming a unit elasticity of private demand to the real interest rate, r^* increases from 0% to 2%. Suppose now that, in response to private demand, the government reduces the primary deficit by 2%, and the multiplier is equal to 1. The result is no change in r^* or in r, and a lower primary deficit. The debt ratio now decreases, other things being equal, by 2% each year. One can think of variations of this scenario. Suppose that the government reduces the primary deficit by only 1%, and the BOJ keeps the nominal rate unchanged. Assume that the resulting overheating leads inflation to be higher by 1%. Assuming debt is nominal, the real value of the debt decreases by 1%; the decrease in the real interest rate by 1% and the decrease in the primary deficit by 1% combine to decrease debt further over time. If the initial debt ratio is 100%, then debt decreases initially by 2% a year.

The third possibility is an increase in aggregate demand in the world, leading to an increase in foreign r^* and r. If we assume that Japanese financial markets are largely integrated, and if the BOJ does not match the increase in foreign r^*, this is likely to lead to a yen depreciation and some induced inflation. Again, the likely expansionary effects of the depreciation (and given that Japanese public debt is not in foreign currency) allow for a decrease in deficits while keeping output at potential. And inflation reduces the real value of the debt, and decreases r, leading to more favorable debt dynamics.

The point of this discussion is not to argue that even with high debt levels there is no danger from higher rates. Indeed, reducing deficits, even if they do not lead to lower output, is difficult to achieve politically and may not happen, leading to questions about debt sustainability.[19] But the danger may be less than is usually argued.

---

18. For reasons we discussed in chapter 5, the government should not offset the full increase in private demand; it should do less, in order to allow for an increase in the neutral rate, and by implication in the policy rate, and give more room for monetary policy. Let me leave this aside in this exercise and assume full offset.

19. In discussing the use of stochastic debt sustainability analysis (SDSA) for assessing debt sustainability in chapter 4, I suggested a two-step approach, doing it first under existing policies and then exploring how the government might react. If rates were

What if private demand remains very weak, forcing large deficits and further increasing debt ratios?

What may be more worrying than strong private demand and pressure on rates is actually the opposite outcome—namely, continued deep private demand weakness, forcing the BOJ to stay at the ELB and requiring deficits so large as to lead to a further steady increase in debt ratios. As the computation above suggests, it would take large deficits to lead to further steady increases in debt ratios, but it cannot be excluded. This forces one to think of other ways to maintain aggregate demand. This in turn takes us to the earlier discussion of what factors might be behind weak private demand and low neutral rates and whether any of them can be affected by policy.

Focusing first on the saving side, I argued in chapter 5 that increases in social insurance, besides being desirable on their own, can decrease the need for precautionary saving and thus increase consumption demand. Although social insurance is already high in Japan, there may be room to do more. Prime Minister Fumio Kishida has proposed expanding retirement insurance for nonregular workers. This may not boost saving very much but goes in the right direction.

Focusing on the investment side, I begin by noting that past public investment has a mixed reputation in Japan, with remembrances of bridges to nowhere. But public investment can take other forms. In particular, as discussed in chapter 5, there may also be a coincidence between the desirability of green investment to fight global warming, and its desirability on macroeconomic grounds. To the extent that public green investment has substantial spillovers to private investment, it may lead to an increase in aggregate demand without the need to run large deficits. And to the extent that investment increases growth in the future—which green investment may not accomplish but other types of public spending (e.g., better child care or measures to increase the fertility rate and reverse the population decline) might—it also can improve debt dynamics by increasing g relative to r.

Given its high debt level, Japan should make it a priority to think about ways, other than deficits, to sustain demand. But it is an important issue for other countries to start exploring as well.

---

to increase and policies were not readjusted, the first step would signal a potential problem; the second step would explore whether and how the government might react and take into account political limits.

6.3 The Biden Bet: *r*, *r**, and *g*

Given the delay between the time a manuscript is finished and the book comes out, it is dangerous to discuss current policies and what they may imply for the future. Here, I shall take the risk and discuss what I call the Biden bet—that is, the very large fiscal package put in place by the Biden administration in early 2021. I shall do so because it shows how to apply the approach developed in chapter 5, as well as the complexities involved in designing fiscal policy in the current environment.

In early March 2020, when the dangers from coronavirus disease 2019 (Covid-19) became clear, the administration of President Donald Trump reacted quickly. It implemented lockdowns and stay-at-home measures that came, however, at a high output cost (GDP went down by 31% at an annual rate in the second quarter of 2020). In parallel, it put in place several large fiscal programs throughout the year: the Coronavirus Preparedness and Response Supplemental Appropriations Act in March 2020 for $192 billion; the Paycheck Protection Program and Health Care Enhancement Act in April for $483 billion; the Coronavirus Aid, Relief, and Economic Security Act (CARES) in June 2020 for $2.3 trillion (which included about $1.0 trillion in loans, half of them potentially forgivable and likely to be forgiven). The Fed decreased the policy rate from 1.5% in February to 0.05% by March 2020. The approach to both monetary and fiscal policy was: "Whatever it takes." Protection of households and firms was the goal, rather than sustaining demand. It led to a large increase in the net debt ratio, from 83% at the end of 2019 to 90% the end of 2020.

As 2020 progressed, the situation improved, with fewer lockdowns and confinements. Medical progress on fighting Covid was rapid. Genetic sequencing was achieved early in the year, and clinical trials of Covid vaccines were started. By December, a number of vaccines were approved and the general assumption became that Covid would be largely under control by mid-2021. The question became how to move from protection to recovery, how best to support demand and go back quickly to potential output. This is what I want to focus on here.

Two major programs were put in place. The first was the Impact Aid Coronavirus Relief Act, put in place by the Trump administration in December 2020 for $870 billion, and then the American Rescue Plan (ARP), put in place in March 2021 by the Biden administration for $1.9 trillion.

This last program, coming on top of the earlier program by the Trump administration, was a major fiscal expansion. Let's do a computation.

Consider first the potential size of the output gap to be filled, as it could be assessed at the time. In January 2020, the unemployment rate had been 3.5%, the lowest since 1953; it could reasonably be taken as being close to the natural unemployment rate. Put another way, in January 2020, output was probably very close to potential. The Congressional Budget Office (CBO) estimated potential real output growth for the earlier years to have been around 1.7%. Assuming that potential output continued to grow at the same rate during 2020, and given that actual real GDP in 2020 Q4 was 2.5% below its level a year earlier, this CBO estimate implied an output gap in 2020 Q4 of 1.7% + 2.5% = 4.2%, or, in nominal terms, about $900 billion.

Given the supply restrictions caused directly or indirectly by Covid-19, it was clear even then that $900 billion was undoubtedly an overestimate of the gap that could be filled by an increase in demand. The pandemic had severely lowered potential output and was likely to continue to do so for at least a good part of at 2021. Supposing, conservatively, that potential output was still down by 1% in 2021 relative to where it would have been absent Covid-19, the output gap that needed to be filled in 2021 by an increase in demand was only $680 billion.

On the demand side, the issue was how much the program would increase aggregate demand. Determining that required assumptions about multipliers. By decomposing the ARP program into its different components and using the set of mean values of multipliers from the Council of Economic Advisers (2014, chap. 3, table 3-5) to assess the likely effect of the program on aggregate demand, this analysis implied an overall multiplier (the ratio of the increase in aggregate demand to the size of the package) equal to 1.2, and thus an increase in spending of $2.1 trillion, so three to four times the estimated size of the output gap.[20] But the degree of uncertainty was very large: The overall multiplier, under the low multiplier estimates, was 0.4; using the high multiplier, it was nearly 2.0. To the effects of the ARP, passed in March 2021, had to be added the effects of the Trump administration program passed earlier, in December 2020, for $870 billion, with similar uncertainty about the relevant multipliers. And yet another source of uncertainty came from the fact that, in 2020, as a

---

20. The details of the computation are given in Blanchard 2021a.

result of the various fiscal programs, households had saved an estimated $1.6 trillion more than usual; how much of it they would spend was very difficult to assess. In any case, even with conservative assumptions about multipliers and about consumption out of accumulated savings, it appeared that the increase in aggregate demand would vastly exceed the estimate of the output gap, leading to overheating.

On monetary policy, the Fed indicated that it would keep rates "low for long," waiting for output to be back at potential and inflation to exceed 2% before increasing the policy rate; meanwhile, the Fed would continue to buy government bonds and mortgage-based securities. To cite from the Federal Open Market Committee (FOMC) statement of July 2021:[21]

> The Committee seeks to achieve maximum employment and inflation at the rate of 2 percent over the longer run. With inflation running persistently below this longer-run goal, the Committee will aim to achieve inflation moderately above 2 percent for some time so that inflation averages 2 percent over time and longer-term inflation expectations remain well anchored at 2 percent. The Committee expects to maintain an accommodative stance of monetary policy until these outcomes are achieved. The Committee decided to keep the target range for the federal funds rate at 0 to 1/4 percent and expects it will be appropriate to maintain this target range until labor market conditions have reached levels consistent with the Committee's assessments of maximum employment and inflation has risen to 2 percent and is on track to moderately exceed 2 percent for some time.

Did this fiscal and monetary policy strategy make sense? (It is not clear that it was a thought-out, coordinated "strategy." It is not clear that the Biden administration intended to achieve substantial overheating, nor that the program was designed in coordination with the Federal Reserve. But we can look at it this way.) In terms of the discussion in chapter 5, one could think of three options open to US policymakers at the start of 2020:

• A minimal approach: Have a fiscal expansion just sufficient to increase the neutral rate r^* back to r_{min}, the ELB rate; equivalently, have a fiscal expansion sufficient to bring output back to potential while keeping the policy rate at the effective lower bound. Anything smaller would be undesirable, leaving a negative output gap. Given the substantial uncertainty,

21. Board of Governors of the Federal Reserve System, "Federal Reserve issues FOMC statement," news release, March 17, 2021, https://www.federalreserve.gov /newsevents/pressreleases/monetary20210317a.htm.

ideally make it partly contingent on the realization of private demand over time to avoid doing too little or too much.

• A more ambitious approach: Have a larger fiscal expansion, thus an increase in the neutral rate r^* above r_{min}, and have the Fed increase the policy rate r in line with the increase in r^* to keep output at potential. We saw in chapter 5, the arguments for such a strategy—namely, giving monetary policy room to react to adverse shocks were they to happen later. Again, design the program to be partly contingent so as to adjust it over time if needed.

• An even more ambitious approach: Have the same fiscal expansion as in the second option, so with an increase in r^* above r_{min}, but have the Fed delay the adjustment of the policy rate r to r^*, thus leading to overheating for some time and a temporary increase in inflation. The potential advantage over the second option, in addition to an implied decrease in the real value of the debt and the effect of a lower real rate for some time on debt dynamics, is to generate an increase in the inflation rate to compensate for an inflation rate below the target in the past, and thus achieve an average inflation rate equal to the target. Again, design the program to be partly contingent.

I believe that the third option is a fair description of the Biden administration and Fed strategy. Proponents argued for the program on four grounds.

First, the overheating would be limited, either because people would not spend much or because potential output was higher than the estimate above. Second, the fiscal expansion following the Global Financial Crisis should have been larger, so the same mistake should not be made again. Third, given the difficulty of achieving the inflation target in the past, more inflation for some time was desirable. Fourth, even if there were overheating, the Phillips curve relation between inflation and unemployment was very flat, so there would be little inflation.

Others, including me, pointed to risks, agreeing about the direction of fiscal policy but worrying about its magnitude.[22] The worry was that private demand could be quite strong on its own, in particular because of the accumulation of excess savings during the pandemic. Another worry was that the program was heavily front-loaded and could not be reduced in size if demand turned out to be too strong. The risk therefore was that there

22. See Blanchard 2021a, and Summers 2021.

would be substantial overheating and that the increase in inflation would be much larger than implied by the historical Phillips curve relation, forcing the Fed to react and increase interest rates more than was intended, at least for some time.

The story is still happening. Nine months later, at the time this is written, where do things stand?

Potential output has turned out to be lower than forecast. Many workers have not returned to work; the participation rate, at 61.9% in December 2021, was up from 60.2% in April 2020 but down from 63.4% in January 2020. Demand has been strong, with an increase in the demand for goods relative to services. The unemployment rate has come down dramatically, from 14.8% in April 2020 to 3.9% in December 2021. A high ratio of vacancies to unemployment and a high quit rate both indicate that the labor market is tight. Strong world demand, partly due to US demand, has led to a large increase in commodity prices, increasing costs of production. Supply chain disruptions, partly due to Covid but mostly due to high demand, have led to shortages and higher prices.

As a result, inflation has increased substantially more than proponents of the program had forecast. As shown in figure 6.4, CPI inflation (measured as quarter over quarter of the previous year) exceeded 5% in 2021 Q3, largely due to the increase in commodity prices. In 2021 Q3, a global commodity price index for the United States was more than 60% higher than a year earlier. And the tight labor market has led to an increase in wage inflation, although so far the increase remains moderate.

What happens next? One can think of two scenarios (assuming that there are no major new disruptions from Covid or other factors).

The first is that participation rates return at least to their pre-Covid levels; that supply chain disruptions disappear; that commodity prices return to lower levels; that private demand weakens, decreasing pressure in the labor market; that productivity growth turns out to be high, reflecting changes in the organization of firms during the crisis and limiting the effects of wage increases back on prices. If so, inflation may naturally return closer to 2%, without the Federal Reserve having to increase the policy rate substantially. Real rates remain low in this scenario.[23]

---

23. As of December 2021, the "dot plot," which plots the forecasts of individual FOMC members for the policy rate, has a median value of 0.75% for the end of 2022 and of 1.5% at the end of 2023.

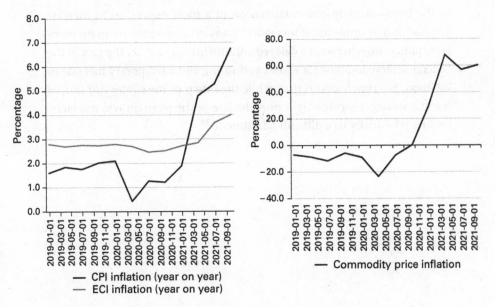

Figure 6.4
Price, wage inflation, and commodity inflation 2019 Q1 to 2021 Q3.
Source: Consumer price index (CPI), employment cost index (ECI), commodity price index, from Federal Reserve Bank of Saint Louis database (FRED).

The second is that these conditions are not met. Participation rates remain lower because, for example, workers who retired early do not go back to the labor market; supply chain disruptions disappear only slowly; private demand remains strong as households spend their accumulated excess savings; wages continue to rise faster because the tight labor market strengthens the bargaining power of workers, and their desire to compensate for the increase in price inflation. In this case, inflation remains high, the Federal Reserve has to increase the policy rate more than it intended, and real rates may be substantially higher for some period of time. This is what I referred to as a potential temporary increase in rates resulting from the Biden stimulus in the conclusion to chapter 3: Even if fundamentals suggest that real rates will remain low over the medium run, they may be much higher for a while because of fiscal policy. I believe this scenario to be more likely than the first.

My purpose in this section was not to give forecasts but to think about the effects of the stimulus program in light of the discussion of fiscal policy in the book—namely, the combination of a fiscal expansion to increase demand and by implication increase r^*, so as to increase the room for monetary policy, together with a delayed adjustment of r to r^* on the part of the Federal Reserve to allow for some overheating and a temporary increase in inflation. My conclusion is that, while the intent of the strategy (if indeed it was a strategy) was the right one, the size of the program was too large, leading potentially to a difficult adjustment.[24]

---

24. This section also leaves aside the likely macroeconomic effects of the two infrastructure programs: the infrastructure plan that has passed Congress and whatever remains of the Build Back Better Plan, if and when negotiations start again. It is too early to know what size they will have together, how they will be financed, and thus whether and how, apart from their direct and positive effects, they may help sustain demand, increase r^* and r, and alleviate ELB constraints in the future.

7 Summary and Open Issues

It has been a long journey. Let me summarize in 10 points what I see as the main argument of the book:[1]

1. For the last 30 years, advanced economies have suffered chronically weak private demand. Or, put another way, strong saving has been chasing weak investment. In addition, there has been a shift in demand toward safe assets.

2. Together, these factors have led to a steady decrease in the neutral rate—the safe rate needed to maintain output at potential. This state of low demand and resulting low neutral rates has been called "secular stagnation."

3. As the neutral rate has decreased, it has crossed two thresholds—first becoming smaller than the growth rate and then occasionally running into the effective lower bound constraint. This has had two major implications for fiscal policy.

4. As the neutral rate has become lower, and in particular lower than the growth rate, the fiscal costs of debt have decreased and, importantly, so have the welfare costs of debt.

5. As the neutral rate has become close to or even lower than the minimum rate implied by the effective lower bound, monetary policy lost much of its room of maneuver, increasing the benefits of using fiscal policy for macro-stabilization.

6. One cannot be sure, but weak private demand and a high demand for safe assets are likely to be with us for some time to come. The US fiscal stimulus of 2021, the resulting overheating, and the risk that higher inflation

---

1. I also made a longer list of 45 takeaways (Blanchard 2021b), but these 10 points will do for the discussion here.

forces the Fed and other central banks to raise interest rates may lead to higher interest rates for awhile. The underlying factors behind the steady decrease in real rates over the last 30 years are still present, however, and suggest a likely return to sustained low rates afterward.

7. Think of two approaches to fiscal policy: First is a "pure public finance" approach, assuming that monetary policy can maintain output at potential and, if debt is perceived as too high, focusing on debt reduction. Second is a "functional finance" approach, assuming that monetary policy cannot be used, focusing instead on macro-stabilization.

8. The right fiscal policy is then a mix of the two, with the relative weights depending on the strength of private demand. If private demand is strong, then fiscal policy can follow mostly pure public finance principles. The weaker private demand, the more the weight should be on functional finance principles and macro-stabilization.

9. The implication of this way of thinking about the right policy is simple: Use fiscal policy so that the neutral rate at least exceeds the effective lower bound constraint by a reasonable margin, to give enough room for monetary policy to sustain output.

10. For the time being, there is no serious risk to debt sustainability in advanced economies. But these risks could arise. On the one hand, if private demand became very strong and the neutral rate increased substantially, debt service would increase; but strong private demand and increased monetary policy room would also allow for fiscal consolidation without adverse effects on output. On the other hand, if private demand became even weaker, then, to keep output at potential, governments might have to run such large deficits that, despite low interest rates, the debt ratio kept increasing. If so, we would have to think of other ways of reacting to acute secular stagnation.

I see this book, and the work by many others on which it builds, as giving a sense of direction—that is, a more active macro-stabilization role for fiscal policy under low rates. Interestingly, this seems also to be the perception of the profession. Surveys of members of the American Economic Association in 1990, 2000, 2010, and 2021 have asked a number of questions about economic issues and policy issues (Geide-Stevenson and La Para Perez 2021). The answers to the questions related to the macro-stabilization role of fiscal policy are given in the table 7.1 below and show a clear positive trend

Table 7.1

		1990	2000	2010	2021
A large budget deficit has an	A	39.5	40.1	29.9	19.7
adverse impact on the economy	AP	46.5	39.8	45.4	41.7
	D	14.1	20.2	24.7	38.6
Management of the cycle should	A		36.0	15.1	12.2
be left to the Fed; activist fiscal	AP		35.6	28.7	21.2
policies should be avoided	D		28.5	56.2	66.6

Notes: The numbers in the table refer to the proportions of respondents (in percent) in each category. "A": agree; "AP": agree with proviso; "D": disagree.

over time in perceptions of both the efficacy and usefulness of activist fiscal policy.

However, I see many open issues: Compared to the granularity of the advice on monetary policy, the general recommendation to use fiscal policy for macro-stabilization is much too general.

If, for example, a fiscal expansion is needed to sustain demand, should it take the form of an increase in spending, a decrease in taxes, or a balanced budget increase? The macro-stabilization approach focuses on the size of the multipliers. The pure public finance approach focuses on the marginal benefits of spending and the marginal costs of taxation and of debt. How should the two be integrated?

I have implicitly assumed that, if there were no effective lower bound (ELB) constraint, macro-stabilization could be left fully to monetary policy, with fiscal policy following pure public finance principles. This is clearly wrong in a number of ways, which have been documented in the literature.

In some dimensions, fiscal policy has an advantage over monetary policy in stabilizing output. The main example is indeed the operation of automatic stabilizers, which act faster than monetary policy can.

While monetary policy is the right instrument from an efficiency point of view,[2] it has other implications that fiscal policy may not have. For example, as has been made clear by the asset price boom of the past few

---

2. In the standard Keynesian or New Keynesian model, the main source of inefficiency is the presence of nominal rigidities, which prevent the correct adjustment of the interest rate to the neutral rate. Thus, the use of the interest rate by the central bank directly addresses and corrects the source of inefficiency.

years, expansionary monetary policy works in part by increasing asset prices and thus by increasing the wealth of already wealthier individuals; while everybody may benefit from the increase in output, some benefit more than others. These distribution effects can potentially be avoided with the use of fiscal policy, which has many more tools at its disposal.

There is still considerable uncertainty about the channels through which monetary policy affects output. To take a current example, how much the Federal Reserve will have to increase the policy rate in order to get inflation down to target is extremely uncertain. Stansbury and Summers (2020) discuss the elasticity of aggregate demand to the interest rate (the slope of the IS curve in the IS-LM model) and argue that this elasticity may sometimes be small.[3]

If there were no ELB constraint and private demand was very weak, the neutral rate, and by implication the actual interest rate, might have to be large and negative. There is some evidence, however, that very low safe rates lead to excessive risk taking and, in turn, to financial instability. If this is the case, this may be an argument for using fiscal policy even if the effective lower bound was irrelevant (say, because of the replacement of money by digital money), allowing for negative interest rates.

I also feel that there is a set of urgent policy issues that need to addressed. Let me take two of them.

The first is how public green investment should be financed. Fighting global warming is clearly one of the major challenges governments are facing, and it has major macroeconomic implications (for a start, see Pisani-Ferry 2021). I have argued that any public green investment with a risk-adjusted social rate of return should be implemented. Some of the measures, such as a carbon tax, may increase fiscal revenues, although some of the revenues will have to be spent to limit adverse distributional effects. But most of the measures will have to be financed either through taxes or through debt. The issue is what that mix should be.

The second urgent issue is how the conclusions about fiscal policy in advanced economies translate to fiscal policy in emerging markets and low income countries. Borrowing rates for both have also come down, and lower rates imply better fiscal dynamics. At the same time, rates remain

---

3. This was indeed part of the argument by Hansen (1939) for secular stagnation and the use of fiscal rather than monetary policy in general.

substantially higher than in advanced economies, many countries borrow in foreign currency and have a larger and more fickle foreign investor base, and many countries have a higher dependence of fiscal revenues on commodity prices; all these factors lead to higher uncertainty and lower debt sustainability. At the same time, too, higher interest rates imply that the effective lower bound is less of a constraint on monetary policy. Many of those countries have levels of debt that are high by historic standards. How much of this book's advice translates to their situation is an urgent question to answer.[4]

4. For a very rough first pass looking at India, see Blanchard, Felman, and Subramanian 2021.

Bibliography

Abel, Andrew, N. Gregory Mankiw, Lawrence Summers, and Richard Zeckhauser. 1989. "Assessing dynamic efficiency: Theory and evidence." *Review of Economic Studies* 56 (1): 1–19.

Adachi, Ko, and Kazuhiro Hiraki. 2021. "Recent developments in measuring inflation expectations." Bank of Japan Research Laboratory Series 21-E-1, June.

Afonso, Antonio, Pedro Gomes, and Philipp Rother. 2011. "Short- and long-run determinants of sovereign debt credit ratings." *International Journal of Finance and Economics* 16: 1–15.

Aguiar, Mark, Manuel Amador, and Christina Arellano. 2021. "Micro risks and Pareto improving policies with low interest rates." NBER Working Paper 28996, July.

Aiyagari, Rao. 1994. "Uninsured idiosyncratic risk and aggregate saving." *Quarterly Journal of Economics* 109 (3): 659–684.

Aldy, Joseph. 2013. "A preliminary assessment of the American Recovery and Reinvestment Act's Clean Energy Package." *Review of Environmental Economics and Policy* 7 (1): 136–155.

Alesina, Alberto, and Silvia Ardagna. 2009. "Large changes in fiscal policy: Taxes versus spending." NBER Working Paper 15438, October.

Ardagna, Silvia. 2018. "Rating sovereigns: More upgrades on the horizon." Goldman Sachs Economics Research Report, March.

Auclert, Adrien, Hannes Malmberg, Frederic Martenet, and Matthew Roglie. 2021. "Demographics, wealth, and global imbalances in the twenty-first century." NBER Working Paper 29161, August.

Backhouse, Roger, and Mauro Boianovsky. 2016. "Secular stagnation: The history of a macroeconomic heresy." *European Journal of the History of Economic Thought* 23 (6): 946–970.

Ball, Laurence, and N. Greg Mankiw. 2021. "Market power in neoclassical growth models." NBER Working Paper 28538.

Barro, Robert. 1974. "Are government bonds net wealth?" *Journal of Political Economy* 82 (6): 1095–1117.

Barro, Robert. 2021. "r minus g." Unpublished manuscript, Harvard University, August.

Barro, Robert, and Jose Ursua. 2011. "Rare macroeconomic disasters." Harvard Department of Economics Working Paper, August.

Batini, Nicoletta, Mario Di Serio, Mattero Fragetta, Giovanni Melina, and Anthony Waldron. 2021. "Building back better: How big are green spending multipliers?" IMF Working Paper.

Benartzi Shlomo, and Richard Thaler. 1995. "Myopic loss aversion and the equity premium puzzle." *Quarterly Journal of Economics* 110 (1): 73–92.

Bénassy-Quéré, Agnes, Markus Brunnermeier, Henrik Enderlein, Emmanuel Farhi, Marcel Fratzscher, Clemens Fuest, Pierre-Olivier Gourinchas, Philippe Martin, Jean Pisani-Ferry, Helene Rey, Isabel Schnabel, Nicolas Véron, Beatrice Weder di Mauro, and Jeromin Zettelmeyer. 2018. "Reconciling risk sharing with market discipline: A constructive approach to Euro Area reform." *CEPR Policy Insight No. 91*, January.

Bernanke, Ben. 2005. "The global saving glut and the US current account deficit." EconPapers No. 77, speech delivered to Board of Governors of the Federal Reserve System, April.

Blanchard, Olivier. 1985. "Debt, deficits, and finite horizons." *Journal of Political Economy* 93 (2): 223–247.

Blanchard, Olivier. 1990. "Comments on 'Can severe fiscal contractions be expansionary? Tales of two small European countries.'" *NBER Macroeconomics Annual* 5: 111–116.

Blanchard, Olivier. 1993. "Movements in the equity premium." *Brookings Papers on Economic Activity* 2: 75–138.

Blanchard, Olivier. 2019a. "Comment on Christina and David Romer, 'Fiscal space and the aftermath of financial crises: How it matters and why.'" *Brookings Papers on Economic Activity* (Spring): 314–321.

Blanchard, Olivier. 2019b. "Public debt and low interest rates." *American Economic Review* 109 (4): 1197–1229.

Blanchard, Olivier. 2021a. "In defense of concerns over the $1.9 trillion relief plan." *Peterson Institute for International Economics*, February.

Blanchard, Olivier. 2021b. "Why low interest rates force us to revisit the scope and role of fiscal policy: 45 takeaways." *Realtime Economic Issues Watch* (blog), *Peterson Institute for International Economics*, December.

Blanchard, Olivier, Josh Felman, and Arvind Subramanian. 2021."Does the new fiscal consensus in advanced economies travel to emerging markets?" PIIE Policy Brief 21-7, March.

Blanchard, Olivier, and Jordi Gali. 2007. "Real wage rigidities and the New Keynesian model." *Journal of Money, Credit and Banking* 39 (1): 35–65.

Blanchard, Olivier, Michael Kister, and Gonzalo Huertas. 2021. "Notes on debt limits, uncertainty, and sudden stops." Unpublished manuscript, work in progress.

Blanchard, Olivier, Alvaro Leandro, and Jeromin Zettelmeyer. 2021. "Redesigning fiscal EU rules. From rules to standards." *Economic Policy* 36 (106): 195–236.

Blanchard, Olivier, and Daniel Leigh. 2013. "Growth forecast errors and fiscal multipliers." *American Economic Review* 103 (3): 117–120.

Blanchard, Olivier, and Lawrence Summers. 2020. "Automatic stabilizers in a low rate environment." *American Economic Review Papers and Proceedings* 110: 125–130.

Blanchard, Olivier, and Takeshi Tashiro. 2019. "Fiscal policy options for Japan." PIIE Policy Brief 19-7, May 2019.

Bohn, Henning. 1998. "The behavior of US public debt and deficits." *Quarterly Journal of Economics* 113: 949–963.

Bomfim, Antulio. 1997. "The equilibrium Fed funds rate and the indicator properties of term-structure spreads." *Economic Inquiry* 35 (October): 830–846.

Borio, Claudio, Piti Disyatat, and Phurichai Rungcharoenkitkul. 2019. "What anchors for the natural rate of interest?" BIS Working Paper 777 March.

Boushey, Heather, Ryan Nunn, and Jay Shambaugh. 2019. "Recession ready: Fiscal policies to stabilize the American economy." *The Hamilton Project, Brookings Institution*, May 16.

Brumm, Johannes, Xiangyu Feng, Laurence Kotlikoff, and Felix Kubler. 2021. "Deficit follies." NBER Working Paper 28952 June.

Brynjolfsson, Erik, and Andrew McAfee. 2014. *The Second Machine Age: Work, Progress, and Prosperity in a Time of Brilliant Technologies*. New York: W.W. Norton.

Buti, Marco. 2021. *The Man Inside: A European Journey through Two Crises*. Milan: Bocconi University Press.

Caballero, Ricardo, Emmanuel Farhi, and Pierre-Olivier Gourinchas. 2017. "The safe asset shortage conundrum." *Journal of Economic Perspectives* 31 (3): 29–46.

Cochrane, John. 2022. *The Fiscal Theory of the Price Level*. Princeton, NJ: Princeton University Press.

Council of Economic Advisers. 2014. Economic Report of the President. Chapter 3. Washington, DC: US Government Printing Office.

Council of Economic Advisers. 2016. "A retrospective assessment of clean energy investment in the Recovery Act," February.

Dechezleprêtre, Antoine, Ralf Martin, and Myra Mohnen. 2017. "Knowledge spillovers from clean and dirty technologies." Grantham Research Institute on Climate Change and the Environment Working Paper 135, October.

Del Negro, Marco, Domenico Giannone, Marco Giannoni MP, and Andrea Tambalotti. 2019. "Global trends in interest rates." *Journal of International Economics* 118: 248–262.

DeLong, Brad, and Lawrence Summers. 2012. "Fiscal policy in a depressed economy." *Brookings Papers on Economic Activity* (Spring): 233–297.

Diamond, Peter. 1965. "National debt in a neoclassical growth model." *American Economic Review* 55 (5): 1126–1150.

Eggertson, Gauti, Neil Mehrotra, and Jacob Robbins. 2019. "A model of secular stagnation; Theory and quantitative evaluation." *American Economic Review* 11 (1): 1–48.

Farhi, Emmanuel, and François Gourio. 2019. "Accounting for macro-finance trends: Market power, intangibles, and risk premia." NBER Working Paper 25282, February.

Farhi, Emmanuel, and Jean Tirole. 2012. "Bubbly liquidity." *Review of Economic Studies* 79:678–706.

Favero, Carlo, Arie Gozluklu, and Andrea Tamoni. 2011. "Demographic trends, the dividend price ratio, and the predictability of long-run stock market returns." *Journal of Financial and Quantitative Analysis* (October): 1493–1520.

Furman, Jason, and Lawrence Summers. 2020. "A reconsideration of fiscal policy in the era of low interest rates." Harvard University Working Paper, November.

Geerolf, François. 2018. "Reassessing dynamic efficiency." UCLA Working Paper, September.

Geide-Stevenson, Doris, and Alvaro La Para Perez. 2021. "Consensus among economists 2020: A sharpening of the picture." Weber State University Working Paper, December.

Giavazzi, Francesco, and Marco Pagano. 1990. "Can severe fiscal contractions be expansionary? Tales of two small European countries." *NBER Macroeconomics Annual* 5: 75–122.

Goode, Ethan, Zheng Liu, and Thuy Lan Nguyen. 2021. "Fiscal multiplier at the zero lower bound in Japan." *Federal Reserve Bank of San Francisco Economic Letter*, May.

Goodhart, Charles, and Manoj Pradhan. 2020. *The Great Demographic Reversal: Ageing Societies, Waning Inequality, and an Inflation Revival*. Cham, Switzerland: Springer.

Gordon, Robert. 2016. *The Rise and Fall of American Growth: The US Standard of Living since the Civil War*. Princeton, NJ: Princeton University Press.

Greenwood, Robin, Samuel Hanson, Joshua Rudolph, and Lawrence Summers. 2014. "Government debt management at the zero lower bound." Hutchins Center on Fiscal and Monetary Policy Working Paper 5, September.

Gutierrez, German, and Thomas Philippon. 2017. "Declining competition and investment in the US." NBER Working Paper 23583.

Hansen, Alvin. 1939. "Economic progress and declining population growth." *American Economic Review* 29:1–15.

Haskel, Jonathan. 2020. "Monetary policy in the intangible economy." *Bank of England*, February.

Hellwig, Martin. 2021. "Safe assets, risky assets, and dynamic inefficiency in overlapping generations economies." Max Planck Institute Working Paper, May.

Holmström, Bengt, and Jean Tirole. 1998. "Private and public supply of liquidity." *Journal of Political Economy* 106 (1): 1–40.

International Energy Agency. 2021. *Net Zero by 2050: A Roadmap for the Global Energy Sector*. Paris: IEA.

International Monetary Fund. 2021. "Review of the debt sustainability framework for market access countries." IMF Policy Paper, January.

Irish Fiscal Advisory Council. 2021. *Fiscal Assessment Report, May*. Dublin: Irish Fiscal Advisory Council.

Ito, Takatoshi, and Takeo Hoshi. 2020. *The Japanese Economy*. 2nd ed. Cambridge, MA: MIT Press.

Kiley, Michael. 2020. "The global equilibrium real interest rate: Concepts, estimates, and challenges." *Annual Review of Financial Economics* 12 (1): 305–226.

Kocherlakota, Narayana. 2021. "Public debt bubbles in heterogenous agent models with tail risk." NBER Working Paper 29138, August.

Krishnamurthy, Arvind, and Annette Vissing-Jorgensen. 2012. "The aggregate demand for treasury debt." *Journal of Political Economy* 120 (2): 233–267.

Krugman, Paul. 1998. "It's baaack: Japan's slump and the return of the liquidity trap." *Brookings Papers on Economic Activity* 2: 137–205.

Laubach, Thomas, and John Williams. 2003. "Measuring the natural rate of interest." *Review of Economics and Statistics* 85 (4): 1063–1070.

Leigh, Daniel, Pete Devries, Charles Freedman, Jaime Guajardo, Douglas Laxton, and Andrea Pescatori. 2010. "Will it hurt? Macroeconomic effects of fiscal consolidation." *World Economic Outlook* (October): 93–124.

Lerner, Abba. 1943. "Functional finance and the federal debt." *Social Research* 10 (1): 38–51.

Lorenzoni, Guido, and Ivan Werning. 2019. "Slow moving debt crises." *American Economic Review* 109 (9): 3229–3263.

Lunsford, Kurt, and Kenneth West. 2019. "Some evidence on secular drivers of US safe real rates." *American Economic Journal: Macroeconomics* 11 (4): 113–139.

Luo, Kevin, Tomoko Kinusaga, and Kai Kajitani. 2020. "Dynamic efficiency in world economy." *Prague Economic Papers* 29 (5): 522–544.

Maravalle, Alessandro, and Łukasz Rawdanowicz. 2020. "How effective are automatic stabilizers in the OECD countries?" OECD Economics Department Working Paper 1635, December.

Martin, Philippe, Jean Pisani-Ferry, and Xavier Ragot. 2021. "Reforming the European fiscal framework." *Les notes du conseil d'analyse économique* 63 (April).

Maruyama, Toshitaka, and Kenji Suganuma. 2019. "Inflation expectations curve in Japan." Bank of Japan Working Paper Series 19-E-6, April.

Masuch, Klaus. 2021. "Monetary, fiscal and financial policy interactions: Conceptual and policy considerations." ECB Working Paper.

Mauro, Paolo, and Jing Zhou. 2021. "$r - g < 0$: Can we sleep more soundly?" *IMF Economic Review* (January 2021): 197–229.

Mehra, Rajnish, and Edward Prescott. 1985. "The equity premium: A puzzle." *Journal of Monetary Economics* 15 (2): 146–161.

Mian, Atif, Ludwig Straub, and Amir Sufi. 2021a. "A goldilocks theory of fiscal policy." Unpublished manuscript, Princeton University, August.

Mian, Atif, Ludwig Straub, and Amir Sufi. 2021b. "What explains the decline in r^*? Rising income inequality versus demographic shifts." Paper prepared for the Jackson Hole Economic Symposium, August.

Michau, Jean-Baptiste. 2020. "Fiscal policy under secular stagnation: An optimal pump priming strategy." Unpublished working paper, December.

Obstfeld, Maurice. 2020. "Global dimensions of US monetary policy." *International Journal of Central Banking* (February): 73–132.

Pethe, Jean-Baptiste. 2021. "The case for higher equilibrium interest rates." *Exane BNP Paribas Economics Research*, August 2021.

Phelps, Edmund. 1961. "The golden rule of accumulation: A fable for growthmen." *American Economic Review* 51 (4): 638–643.

Piketty, Thomas. 2014. *Capital in the Twenty-First Century*. Cambridge, MA: Harvard University Press.

Pisani-Ferry, Jean. 2021. "Climate policy is macroeconomic policy, and the implications will be significant." PIIE Policy Brief 21-20, August.

Platzer, Josef, and Marcel Peruffo. 2021. "Secular drivers of the natural rate of interest in the United States." Brown University Working Paper, April.

Posen, Adam. 1999. "Implementing Japanese recovery." PIIE Policy Brief 99-1, January.

Rachel, Łukasz, and Lawrence Summers. 2019. "On secular stagnation in the industrialized world." NBER Working Paper 26198, August.

Ramey, Valerie. 2019. "Ten years after the financial crisis: What have we learned from the renaissance in fiscal research? *Journal of Economic Perspectives* 33 (2): 89–114.

Reis, Ricardo. 2020. "The constraint on public debt when $r < g$ but $g > m$." London School of Economics Working Paper, December.

Reis, Ricardo. 2022. "The fiscal revenue from public borrowing." London School of Economics Working Paper, January.

Rogoff, Kenneth. 2017. *The Curse of Cash: How Large-Denomination Bills Aid Crime and Tax Evasion and Constrain Monetary Policy*. Princeton, NJ: Princeton University Press.

Romer, David. 2012. *Macroeconomics*. New York: McGraw-Hill.

Romer, David, and Christina Romer. 2019. "Fiscal space and the aftermath of financial crises: How it matters and why." *Brookings Papers on Economic Activity* (Spring): 239–331.

Schmelzing, Paul. 2020. "Eight centuries of global real interest rates, R-G, and the 'suprasecular' decline, 1311–2018." Bank of England Staff Working Paper 845.

Schnabel, Isabel. 2021. "Unconventional fiscal and monetary policy at the zero lower bound." Speech at the Third Annual Conference of the European Fiscal Board, Frankfurt am Main, February 26.

Springel, Katalin. 2021. "Network externality and subsidy structure in two-sided markets: Evidence from electric vehicle incentives." *American Economic Journal: Economic Policy* 13 (4): 393–432.

Standard and Poor's. 2019. How We Rate Sovereigns.

Stansbury, Anna, and Lawrence Summers. 2020. "The end of the golden age of banking? Secular stagnation is about more than the zero lower bound." Harvard University Working Paper.

Summers, Lawrence. 1990. "What is the social return to capital investment?" In *Growth, Productivity, and Unemployment, Essays in Honor of Robert Solow*, edited by Peter Diamond, 113–141. Cambridge, MA: MIT Press.

Summers, Lawrence. 2014. "Reflections on the new secular stagnation hypothesis." In *Secular Stagnation: Facts, Causes and Cures*, edited by C. Teulings and R. Baldwin, 27–38. London: CEPR.

Summers, Lawrence. 2016. "Secular stagnation and monetary policy." *Federal Reserve Bank of Saint Louis Review* 98 (2): 93–110.

Summers, Lawrence. 2021. "The Biden stimulus is admirably ambitious. But it brings some big risks, too." *Washington Post*, February 4.

Timbeau, Xavier, Elliot Aurissergues, and Éric Heyer. 2021. "Public debt in the 21st century: Analyzing public debt dynamics with debtwatch." OFCE Policy Brief, October.

Ubide, Angel. 2017. *The Paradox of Risk: Leaving the Monetary Policy Comfort Zone.* Washington, DC: Peterson Institute for International Economics.

Von Weizsacker, Carl Christian, and Hagen Kramer. 2021. *Saving and Investment in the Twenty-First century: The Great Divergence*. Cham, Switzerland: Springer.

Wicksell, Knut. 1936. *Interest and Prices*. Translation by R. F. Kahn of the 1898 edition. London: Macmillan.

Woodford, Michael. 1990. "Public debt as private liquidity." *American Economic Review Papers and Proceedings* 80 (2): 382–388.

Zenios, Stavros, Andrea Consiglio, Marialena Athanasopoulou, Edmund Moshammer, Angel Gavilan, and Aitor Erce. 2021. "Risk management for sustainable sovereign debt financing." *Operations Research* 69 (3): 755–773.

Index